WINE COUNTRY USA

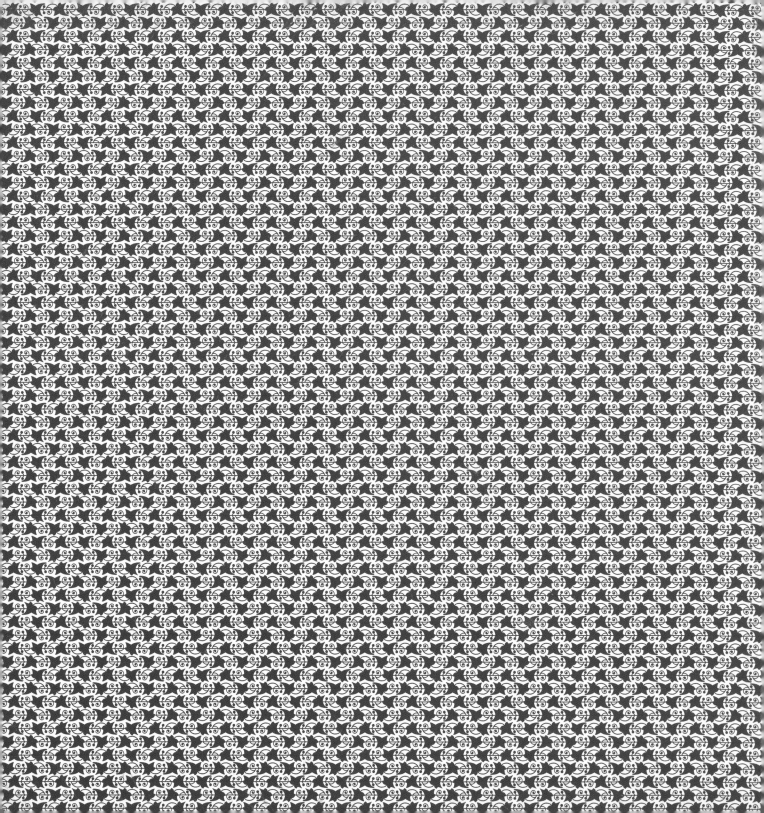

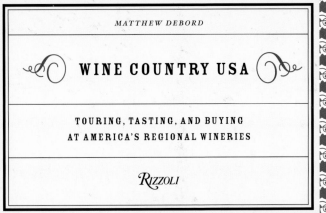

MATTHEW DEBORD

WINE COUNTRY USA

TOURING, TASTING, AND BUYING
AT AMERICA'S REGIONAL WINERIES

RIZZOLI

First published in the United States of America in 2005

Rizzoli International Publications, Inc.

300 Park Avenue South

New York, NY 10010

www.rizzoliusa.com

© 2005 Matthew DeBord

2005 2006 2007 2008 / 10 9 8 7 6 5 4 3 2 1

Printed in China

ISBN: 0-8478-2670-8

Library of Congress Catalog Control Number: 2004096977

∿∾ *PAGE VI:* A cellar door at Spicewood Vineyards in Texas.

∿∾ *PAGE VIII:* Barboursville Vineyards in Virginia.

FOR LUCIA

CONTENTS

Introduction 1

CHAPTER 1 Long Island 6

CHAPTER 2 The Finger Lakes 28

CHAPTER 3 The Mid-Atlantic 48

CHAPTER 4 The Southeast 66

CHAPTER 5 The Midwest 86

CHAPTER 6 The Southwest 102

CHAPTER 7 The Mountain States 122

CHAPTER 8 Oregon 138

CHAPTER 9 Washington 162

CHAPTER 10 California 180

APPENDIX Glossary 208

Acknowledgments 211

Schedule of Festivals 212

Listing of Stores 212

Index 214

INTRODUCTION

IF YOU'RE LIKE MOST WINE DRINKERS, you've probably never once in your life considered uncorking a port from Texas, a Chardonnay from Virginia, or a sparkling wine from Michigan.

Oh, what you're missing out on!

In the past ten years, the American regional winemaking scene has exploded. There are currently wineries in all of the lower forty-eight states, and even in Hawaii. From coast to coast, it seems, there are plenty of people who not only want to drink wine, but want to make it as well.

But that's not the real story. The truth is that, in the past decade, American regional winemaking has surged ahead in terms of quality. Old-timers will recall, way back in the 1960s, when it was considered déclassé to serve a *California* wine. In those days, after all, it was believed that wines from Europe, and France in particular, were just so much better.

Well, fast forward a quarter century and look at California now (and we will, in some depth). The Golden State is a titan of the international wine scene. It is America's megaregion, its wine country par excellence. Not far behind are Oregon and Washington, states that were once also pooh-poohed. How long will it be before another state breaks out?

Not long, if my judgment is worth anything. Right now I'd put my money on Virginia, but Texas could wind up being the winner. Or New York could reclaim some of its vanished glory. It's not exactly a crapshoot, but there are a number of players at the table right now.

And many of them are cranking out really, really good wines. The difference from the old, mom-and-pop days of American regional winemaking, when you were just as likely to encounter a bottle of strawberry wine as a bottle of Merlot, is that most serious vintners have begun to move

A SUBJECTIVE LIST

Here is a highly debatable list, in no particular order, of the best wines representing the top ten regions in America today.

1. ROBERT MONDAVI RESERVE CABERNET (CA)

2. BEAUX FRÈRES BEAUX FRÈRES VINEYARD PINOT NOIR (OR)

3. LEONETTI MERLOT (WA)

4. RED NEWT RIESLING DRY RESERVE (NY—FINGER LAKES)

5. WÖLFFER ESTATE SELECTION CHARDONNAY (NY—LONG ISLAND)

6. VALHALLA VINEYARDS GOTTERDAMMERUNG (VA)

7. BECKER VINEYARDS VINTAGE PORT ESTATE BOTTLED (TX)

8. CHADDSFORD PHILIP ROTH VINEYARD CHARDONNAY (PA)

9. L. MAWBY BLANC DE BLANC (MI)

10. PLUM CREEK CELLARS CABERNET FRANC (CO)

toward vinifera grapes in a big way. Vinifera just means that the grapes that go into the wines are of the so-called noble varieties—for example, Cabernet Sauvignon, Pinot Noir, and Chardonnay—all the grapes (and wines) that are familiar to drinkers of California wines. California was always vinifera-centric; that's why its wine industry achieved escape velocity so quickly. The Europeans had to take the grapes that went into the wines seriously.

Vinifera means risk. The grapes can be much, much harder to cultivate, and in order to turn them into good wines, a winemaker must do things like reduce vineyard fruit yields and buy expensive barrels (for aging) and engage in a whole host of other credit-savaging, anxiety-inducing tactics.

Of course, if you do this right—if you have confidence in yourself—you get to be the next California, or Oregon, or Washington. Payday!

Increasingly, they're doing it right in all sorts of places no one expected. Colorado? Missouri? Ohio? North Carolina? Hardly the stuff of dreamily romantic wine-country travelogues, eh? Until now! Because *Wine Country USA* is going to deliver the entire exciting tapestry of upcoming American wine regions—plus stalwart California, *plus* the extremely hip Pacific Northwest—in one gorgeous package.

Many of America's wine regions have all manner of dedicated, lively, and insightful personalities committed to the life of the vine. And where there's wine, there's generally an elegant lifestyle to go along with it. Good wine typically attracts good restaurants, hotels, resorts, spas—if it has happened in, say, the neighborhood of the Napa Valley, chances are it will happen, in one form or another, in a wine region near you. For whatever reason, talented chefs like to congregate around talented winemakers. The two professions, though not as similar as they might initially seem (working in a cellar and working in a kitchen both involve a certain amount of gourmet biochemistry, but the comparisons become strained after that), tango together beautifully.

In many ways, the current state of America's regional wine scene resembles the adolescence of no-less a wine-producing juggernaut than Italy. Thirty or forty years ago, Italian wines were widely regarded as being tasty underperformers. Romantically, many visitors to Italy noticed that every region in the country seemed to produce its own unique wine. Some were delicious, many were awful. Fast forward a few decades—Italy now produces some of the world's most exciting and fashionable wines. And plenty of these bottlings hail from former backwaters, such as Puglia and Sicily. All it took was plants, money, patience, and time.

Traveling America's wine regions is a tremendous way to spend a vacation, a long weekend, or even just a quick jaunt on a Saturday. You can cross the continent (depending on where you live) or pile into the Buick—it doesn't matter; you're almost guaranteed a good time. I favor driving as much as possible in wine country. Some folks would rather charter a limo or ride bikes. Regardless, the maps in the book should help you get around. But remember: Spit! Don't swallow if you plan on motoring from winery to winery.

As you move through *Wine Country USA,* you'll discover that American wine is as much about American winemakers as it is about the bottles of stuff you actually drink. Check out the various personalities that we've profiled in the winery descriptions; that's where the real inspiration is to be found. The classic American spirit of independence finds a new life among these often gutsy and resourceful pioneers.

Still, you want to drink some wine, right? For each chapter, you'll find a rundown of "Labels to Look For." In most cases, these are wines that you should be able to either pick up at the wineries, or purchase online (see the sources section at the back of the book). Some wineries that we feature in the "Tasting Trails" do not have wide distribution, so labels for those are not included here, although of course that does not mean you shouldn't buy bottles from them. And if you get confused by the terminology, even though it's been kept to a minimum, consult the glossary at the back of the book.

Drinking American regional wines at home is a great way to learn about the wines that are produced in your part of the country; plenty of wine shops have begun to carry at least a small amount of the local juice. Of course, there's no substitute for visiting the wineries themselves for several reasons. First, you get to size up the seriousness of the operation. In my experience, there are two different signals that you'll find quality in the bottle: (a) a bare bones facility (this tells you that here it's all about the winemaker and his or her craft); or (b) a healthy presence of advertising, in addition to the wines offered for tastings. See a lot of T-shirts, hats, and assorted promotional items? Excellent. This means the winery is serious about pushing its product to the next level. Even better is the presence of local artisanal foods for sale (cheese, breads, sausages, you name it—whatever the area specializes in). On the other hand, if you see only fruit wines and odd bric-a-brac, the odds are pretty good that you've entered a vinous hustle: a tasting room set up to cater entirely to tourists rather than wine lovers. Another, yet more rare signal of quality, is the presence of estate-grown labels. A surprising number, in fact the vast majority, of wineries in the U. S. depend on obtaining grapes from other vineyards. This does not necessarily mean bad quality; adding an off-site grape to the mix may provide just the balance needed. However, a winery that goes to the trouble of producing a wine made only with grapes from its fields is a winery committed to quality. Bear in mind that in a very established and successful winemaking state like California, these guidelines are all modified. It's like visiting New York City as opposed to Oxford, Mississippi.

Frequently, you'll get to meet the winemaker. This is a great opportunity. Winemakers are often very interesting people. And even if they aren't, they tend to be extremely passionate about what they do. Sure, they'll occasionally drone on and on about vine spacing, hang times, sugar and ripeness levels, and the like. But they'll also speak of their spiritual relationship to their earth, about how wine is bottled poetry, and about their almost universal love of family. You can do a hell of a lot worse that to emulate vintner values. Besides, a half-hour winery and vineyard tour is worth at least as much as several wine classes, just because you get to see what a fermentation tank looks like, get to spit a barrel sample of Chardonnay on the cellar floor, or get the chance to taste a Zinfandel grape fresh from the vine.

Buying wines at regional wineries can be tricky. Obviously, it's best to taste first. It's also considered good form, if the winery doesn't charge for the tasting (or only charges for tastes of its best wines), to purchase a bottle before you leave. (It's your choice whether you fill the truck with a mixed case of wine or limit yourself to three or four wineries, thereby also limiting your take of bottles.) As a general rule, it's best to drink the wines you buy right away. The vast majority of American regional wines, and even most wines from California, Washington, and Oregon, are not meant to age. And what about price? Well, you might receive a slight discount for buying wines at the winery, or for buying six to twelve bottles. Discounts steepen if the winery is trying to get rid of old stock. Sometimes, you can make out like a bandit. By and large, however, I think you should spend no more than $20 to $30 and no less than $10 per bottle. That will keep you away from bad wines, which tend to be severely underpriced, but not get you into the realm of price gouging, a common—and perfectly understandable—practice at many wineries. Why is price-goug-ing acceptable? Because for a small winery to produce a wine worth more than $30, incredible risks have to be taken. There's no way for regional wineries to push the envelope—and sustain investment in their improvement—without jacking up prices on their top wines. Over time, given success, these prices ought to come down.

Even if you do come across a dud now and then, it's the journey itself that makes it all worthwhile. Treat American wine country as a process of discovery; you never know just what you'll turn up—maybe even in your own virtual back-yard. Now, are you ready for some American wine? Then start your engine, and turn the pages.

[A VERY GOOD YEAR]

AMERICAN VINTAGES

For regional American winemaking, vintage is not of the same importance as it is for, say, Bordeaux or Tuscany. Those locales have so thoroughly established their viticulture that "good" years and "bad" years can be immensely significant, in terms of both quality and—to be truthful—investment potential. The obvious exception is, of course, California, and especially the Napa Valley, which has such a reputation that it can compete with the planet's best. However, Washington and Oregon are coming on strong (Oregon in particular is on a run of solid vin-tages since the late 1990s). But if you are forward thinking, you can keep an eye out for the following vintages from the follow-ing regions.

CALIFORNIA, NAPA VALLEY: 1994 and 1997 are the two great vintages in recent years. The Cabernets are magnificent. 1999 shows promise, as does 2001.

OREGON: In Pinot Noir, nothing bad since 1998. 1999s are tops right now.

WASHINGTON STATE: 1999, for Cabernet and Merlot.

LONG ISLAND: 2001 is a year to look for. Merlot and Chardonnay are the stars.

THE FINGER LAKES: 2001 was also a superb vintage upstate. Focus on Riesling.

TEXAS: Look for wines from 1999–2002. Avoid older wines. Reds are best.

VIRGINIA: 2001 and later. Older wines may lack fruit.

MICHIGAN: Seek out nonvintage sparkling wines.

[AT A GLANCE: LONG ISLAND]

CENTRAL ROADS: Route 25 (North Fork); Route 27 (South Fork)

TOWNS TO VISIT: Sag Harbor, Southampton, Easthampton, Greenport

LOCAL FLAVORS:
Long Island ducks are legendary, but the region also gets some of the
best fish in the world. Bluefish and striped bass ("blues" and "stripers,"
in local parlance) run in the spring and summer. There is also an
abundance—though not what there once was—of oysters and clams.

AVERAGE BOTTLE PRICE: $15

BEST TIME TO VISIT: May–October

WINERIES: Thirty-plus

ACRES OF VINES: 3,000

YEARLY WINE PRODUCTION:
1,200,000 gallons

TOP WINES: Merlot, Cabernet Franc, Chardonnay

WEBSITE: www.liwines.com

THE BOTTOM LINE:
Because it's only about 100 miles from New York City, Long Island is closer to the
major wine market than any other U. S. region—a huge advantage.

CHAPTER ONE

LONG ISLAND

RISING IN THE EAST

NEW YORK calls itself the Empire State and, as visitors to New York City routinely note, the locals do not lack for pride. Loud, aggressive pride. Pride to burn. However, until recently, New York seemed to have been quite happy to let other parts of the country steal its winemaking thunder.

Odd, really, as New York was where winemaking in America got its start hundreds of years ago. For most of America's history, it was New York, not California, that led the nation in wine production, until the California wine boom began in earnest, in the 1970s.

Although New York still ranks second overall in terms of U.S. wine output, it now trails California by a wide margin when it comes to wine-industry bragging rights. There are some who maintain that New York never really recovered from Prohibition. But the truth is that New York's early domination of the American wine scene was some-

thing of a fluke, because it was not based on high-quality wines. And when consumers eventually got wise, in the 1970s and '80s, to the new international styles of wine, based mainly on French-grape varieties such as Cabernet Sauvignon and Chardonnay, New York's alternately quaint and volume-oriented wine business began to look very anachronistic.

New Yorkers don't like to play catch-up, but by the 1980s, that's exactly the position they were in. By this time, California was firmly ensconced as the foremost U.S. wine-making state. Oregon and Washington, pursuing an all-premium model, had come on strong. New York, with its lack of solid experience with international vinifera-grape varieties and its history of cranking out gallons of indifferent wines—produced from a hodgepodge of vinifera and native-variety grapes—needed to get its act together, and fast.

〜⚭ Vines, heavy with fruit, wait for harvest at Wölffer Estate.

Even though Long Island isn't nearly as evolved as California in terms of wine-country tourism, the proximity of the Hamptons, New York City's luxurious beachfront getaway, means that there's no shortage of hotels and restaurants on the South Fork. The picturesque old whaling village of Sag Harbor, with its historic **WHALING MUSEUM** (200 Main St., 631-725-0770), is worth a visit. Intrepid explorers will want to trek all the way out to the tip of the South Fork and visit the **MONTAUK POINT LIGHTHOUSE**, which has been in business since 1796 (Route 27, 631-668-2544, above). In the town of Riverhead, closer to the "hinge" between the North and South Forks, families will enjoy a day at **ATLANTIS MARINE WORLD**, a superb aquarium and zoo with indoor and outdoor exhibits (431 East Main St., 631-208-9200).

Along came Long Island. Formerly, winemaking in New York had been focused in two fairly old-fashioned regions: the Hudson Valley and the Finger Lakes. Of these, the Finger Lakes created superior wines, but it had been through a series of boom-and-bust cycles that left its burgeoning premium-wine business shell-shocked and willing to over-extend. Many vintners were happy to pursue a tasting-room economy, never venturing far from home, devoting no money to marketing, and continuing to churn out vatfuls of popular sweet wines that had a devoted local following but stood no chance of impressing wine critics.

The Hudson Valley had fewer quality wineries, and unlike the Finger Lakes, which could boast a signature grape, Riesling, was encumbered by a tradition of part-time vintners and offbeat hybrid grapes that, by the late '90s, no one had any familiarity with anymore: Baco Noir for example, and Seyval Blanc, among others. It yielded passable wines, but forget about competing with California Chards and Cabs.

NEW YORK'S NAPA NEXT DOOR

Into this relative void moved Long Island, whose wine industry was infantile by comparison with the Finger Lakes and the Hudson Valley. The first proper winery was established by the Hargraves in 1973 (there had been premium grape cultivation in the region before that, however.) Geographically, Long Island broke down into two main areas, each of which would later be granted American Viticultural Area (AVA) status by the U.S. government. The

North Fork stretched from the town of Riverhead northeast to Greenport; to the north was Long Island Sound, and to the south, Peconic Bay. The South Fork, with fewer wineries, had the Atlantic Ocean to the south and was better known for the Hamptons, a cluster of eastward-marching enclaves of wealth and leisure. The North Fork was rural; the South Fork was fashionable. But together, these two very different places formed the accidental vanguard of the resurgent New York wine industry.

Matters were profoundly disorganized at first, based more on the passions of a few pioneers, rather than on any sort of coherent master plan. For starters, Long Island's topography did not suggest "wine country" to anyone. It consisted mainly of flat former potato and sod farms. The artist Willem de Kooning was said to have been attracted to the region because it reminded him of his native Dutch lowlands.

Now, flat is easy, as far as planting vineyards goes, but most high-end wine producers these days like to see hillsides; they're considered to be better for "stressing" grapes, thus improving fruit quality. Winemakers also like to see a predictable, borderline harsh climate, based on hot days, cool nights, and limited rain. Long Island's immediate problems were manifold: no hills, humid summers, nights that are as hot as the days, an intemperate maritime climate that could deliver as much rain as sunshine, and—just to top things off—the possibility of a Category 5 hurricane every decade or so.

Boxes of recently harvested grapes at Wölffer Estate.

[WHAT'S IN A NAME]

THE AMERICAN WINE LABEL

Almost to a tee, American winemakers have followed California's compelling lead and labeled their wine varietally. This means that the standard American wine label takes the name of the wine from the name of the grape that makes up of the majority (at least 75 percent) of the wine's blend. For example: Cabernet Sauvignon, Merlot, Chardonnay, Sauvignon Blanc. Wineries in the country's most prestigious regions now also typically specify the wine's AVA (American Viticultural Area) or appellation. Think: Napa Valley, Sonoma, Willamette Valley, or North Fork of Long Island. The idea is that these AVAs have special qualities that consumers will find desirable. Beyond that, there are proprietary wines to deal with. These are wines that are defined by a name rather than a varietal. Famous examples include Joseph Phelps Insignia, Opus One, and Caymus Conundrum. Some wineries put the name of the vineyards from which the grapes were sourced on the label. This is an additional expression of quality, for connoisseurs who are concerned with terroir. Something like the legendary Heitz Martha's Vineyard Cabernet is a fine example. When you get right down to it, an American wine label is a very simple, straightforward document. It is, however, becoming more complicated every year, as American wine improves in quality across the board.

What Long Island did have going for it was, in this order, lots of money and a proximity to New York City. It seemed that, just as wine-country tourism was taking hold among America's upper classes, the East Coast cultural and financial elite decided they should have their very own Napa next door. It took a decade or so, but by the early '90s, the Long Island wine industry was off and running. These days the wine trail out here can get pretty crowded on summer weekends.

Now there are more than two dozen wineries on both the North and South Forks. The signature varietal is Merlot. This is both a triumph of marketing and of chutzpah. Red grapes such as Cabernet Sauvignon and Zinfandel, which flourish in California, don't do well on Long Island. Cabernet especially tends to deliver weak wines with pronounced "green" flavors. Merlot does substantially better. In fact, it tends to ripen more slowly here, thus developing more complexity. Long Island Merlot may provide the best argument against the now-common complaint that American Merlots are flabby and uninspiring.

BIG APPLE BORDEAUX

Long Island winemakers are quick to point out that their region lies on roughly the same latitude as Bordeaux and so should be counted on to produce world-class Merlot, given enough expertise in the vineyard and the cellar. However, wine is made in quite a different way in Bordeaux than on Long Island, and trying to reproduce Bordeaux style exactly is probably impossible here. Long Islanders should instead be pleased with the version of Merlot they've staked out already. With the exception of Cabernet Franc (another Bordeaux grape, by the way), which has turned in some impressive recent results, Merlot looks to be the grape on which Long Island wants to bet the farm.

Ten years ago, this was a no-brainer. America was then preparing to go Merlot gaga. The wine rapidly became, and remains, the country's favorite red. Long Island, with a combination of sensibility and luck, was bringing Merlot to market (albeit a local market). Furthermore, Long Island Merlot didn't suffer from the same critical problems as other U.S. versions of the wine: It showcased nuance, acidity, and lighter fruit. In bad years, it could be dreadful, tasting weedy and tart. But in good years, the fruit was nice and round, backed up by a refreshing acidic kick. With hundreds of restaurants in the New York metropolitan area, a perfect strategy presented itself: market Long Island Merlot as a food-friendly alternative to juicier, but less complex, Merlots from California. The slogan could have been "New York: Our Wines Are Smarter."

However, production did not come without some early screwups. Some winemakers got too enthusiastic with powerful American oak barrels and obliterated good fruit in their wines. Others needed to improve their work in the vineyard. But over time, some competitive Merlots were bottled on both Forks. Now is the time when Long Island is truly coming into its own.

NEW YORK

Vineyards at the Galluccio Family wineries, formerly the Gristina Winery, on the North Fork of Long Island, where there are fewer celebrities and more room for spacious vineyards than on the busy South Fork, home of the Hamptons.

LONG ISLAND

TASTING TRAIL

East Hampton

114

To Montauk

Shelter Island

25

Sag Harbor

Wölffer

Sagg Rd.

Greenport

79

27

Noyack Bay

Sagaponack

Channing Daughters

Bridgehampton

Scuttle Hole Rd.

Little Peconic Bay

Lenz

Raphael

Water Mill

Bedell Cellars

Duck Walk

Castello
di Borghese

Cutchogue

Galluccio Estates

Southampton

Mattituck

Great Peconic Bay

Long Island Sound

25

Shinnecock Bay

Atlantic Ocean

24

27

Schneider

Riverhead

N

0   5 Miles

The winemaking facilities at Castello di Borghese.

CASTELLO DI BORGHESE
VINEYARD & WINERY

This is where it all began in 1973—the Long Island wine industry. Louisa Hargrave, the former owner, has written a book about the adventure of starting up a winery, but for the Italian prince, Marco Borghese, who purchased the property in 1999, the adventure has just begun. The stars of the show here, wine-wise, are the region's signatures: Chardonnay and Merlot. Reserve bottlings of both mean that North Fork fans can find real quality. This winery can't match some of the North Fork showplaces for opulence. But it still has a pleasant, homey quality. Cozy rather than vast, with a small tasting room and a modest display of wines, it reassures with Old School reserve.

ROUTE 48

CUTCHOGUE, NEW YORK

631-734-5111

WWW.CASTELLODIBORGHESE.COM

BEDELL CELLARS

This winery is well known largely thanks to its namesake Kip Bedell's winemaking talent, especially with Merlot, Long Island's signature varietal. Several years ago, Bedell sold the operation to Michael Lynne, a New York–based film producer who proceeded to revamp the winery while still keeping Bedell in charge of the winemaking. The result is a much more airy and sophisticated tasting room than what Bedell veterans were used to. The old facility was rustic and barnlike, while the new one seems filled with light—the better to illuminate Lynne's world-class collection of contemporary art. However, unlike some other new wineries, which borrow from European motifs, the face-lifted Bedell Cellars seeks to emulate the dominant architectural modes of Long Island's East End. The roster of wines runs from the basic, everyday Main Road Red, straight on up to the $30 Merlot Reserve. Now that's not exactly a bargain, given that Long Island Merlots can be a bit temperamental, depending on the vagaries of weather. But bear in mind that Bedell isn't a California or Australian superproducer, cranking out gallons of juicy, jammy wine. It only does about eighty-five hundred cases per year here, red and white. On Long Island, such limited production means that, in order to continue to beef up quality, a winery must

36225 MAIN ROAD, ROUTE 25

CUTCHOGUE, NY 11935

631-734-7537

WWW.BEDELLCELLARS.COM

~~⊛ *TOP:* The lush soil of Bedell Vineyards makes it ideal for growing roses as well as grapes.

~~⊛ *BOTTOM:* Bedell's facilities are bright with color, thanks to their well-landscaped grounds.

~~⊛ *OPPOSITE:* A vineyard row at Raphael, wide enough to allow for the tractors used in harvesting the grapes.

charge a decent price for what it considers to be its premium wines. If you take into account the amount of wine that gets sold out of the tasting room alone each year, it seems that Bedell's supporters are happy to pay for the pleasure. His low-key manner ensures their loyalty. Not only is he commonly regarded as one of the region's top winemakers, he also can boast the lowest golf handicap among Long Island vintners. Bedell is a no-nonsense guy. While some winemakers, following success, can overindulge their egos, Bedell has remained as unpretentious as he was the day he first opened his then rather rudimentary winery on the North Fork's Main Road.

RAPHAEL

This stunning, faux-Tuscan showplace toward the end of Main Road is owned by John Petrocelli, who made his money in the construction business. His experience in the building trades is hard to miss inside this vast winery, with its heavy, lofty timbers, wrought-iron detailing, marble fireplaces, and soaring rooftop cupola. The passion here is for Merlot and, a small amount of Sauvignon Blanc notwithstanding, nothing else. Plans are to keep production limited to no more than fifteen thousand cases per year, thus ensuring quality. The range of wines is also streamlined, with entry-level bottling starting at $15 and the top-of-the-line Merlot coming in at $38. Given that some North Fork tasting rooms can get pretty cozy on a balmy Saturday in September, I've come to appreciate Raphael's indoor acreage, where you can really spread out. Two sights not to miss: the view of the winery's jacketed stainless-steel fermentation tanks, which can be viewed through a window that affords a glimpse of the cellar; and the massive, sloping crush pad that descends from the edge of the vineyards. A lot of engineering went into making this place the best winery it could be, and my advice is to take some time to appreciate it. Winemaker Richard Olsen Harbich is as dedicated as they come, and is rapidly becoming one of the region's true Merlot experts.

39390 MAIN ROAD, ROUTE 25
PECONIC, NY 11958
631-765-1100
WWW.RAPHAELWINE.COM

~~~∞ A building on the Galluccio
grounds.

LENZ

For more than a decade now, Lenz has been able to announce itself as the North Fork's premier artisanal winery. It produces a wide variety of different wines, both reds and whites, but the guts of the operation are its rich, highly extracted Merlots. They put me in the mind of wines from the southern Rhône, so dense and brooding they can be. Lenz has been the venue for several yearly Long Island megatastings, where oenophiles can sample the best the region has to offer, both in terms of wine and food. Winemaker Eric Fry is something of a hippie mad scientist, endlessly experimenting with new wine styles and grape varieties. The winery itself is pure North Fork anti-Hamptons, anti-fashion—rustic and unpretentious, where Fry can often be found hanging around the tasting bar.

MAIN ROAD, ROUTE 25

PECONIC, NY 11958

631-734-6010

WWW.LENZWINE.COM

GALLUCCIO FAMILY WINERIES

Vince Galluccio is a hefty former telecommunications executive who has invested heftily in this property, formerly known as Gristina. When Galluccio purchased the estate in 2000, he paid $5.5 million—at that point the highest price a Long Island winery had ever garnered. He immediately set about making improvements to both the winery's viticulture and its enology, including the hiring of well-traveled, and justifiably famous, French winemaker Michel Rolland as a consultant. Galluccio was fortunate in that Gristina already had one of the best winemaking facilities in the region; prior to the arrival of Raphael, it probably was the most technologically advanced. The winemaking team here is an unusual and borderline eccentric bunch. They favor a sort of Franco-American hybrid in the styles of wine they produce. This translates into a preference for the crisply acidic over the full-blown and fruity—a lucky thing, as the North Fork isn't exactly Napa when it comes to weather. Which isn't to say that they can't also produce powerful wines; they can, but the sort of monster reds generated in California and Australia just isn't their forte. Galluccio's output consists of juicy Merlots, a certain amount of firm, somewhat immature-tasting

24385 MAIN ROAD, ROUTE 25

CUTCHOGUE, NY 11935

631-734-7089

WWW.GALLUCCIOWINERIES.COM

Cabernet Sauvignon, and Chardonnays that fit the North Fork image: somewhere between fruit-bomb Sonoma examples and the less-forthcoming products of Burgundy.

WÖLFFER ESTATE

I'm a real Wölffer partisan, for two reasons. First, this is easily the most inviting and beautiful winery on all of Long Island, the new showplaces on the North Fork included. Owner Christian Wölffer has brought a country gentleman's eye to the project. Wölffer, a German-born financier, established a residence in tony East Hampton in the 1980s, mainly so that he could pursue one of his many passions, horses. Now, of course, Wölffer is far better known for his wine than his horses. Reason number two is winemaker Roman Roth, who, across the board, is the most skilled vintner in the region. A transplant from Germany, Roth makes a wide variety of different wines, from a breezy, bargain summer rosé that flies out of the tasting room, to a robust Bordeaux-style red that sells for $100 and is produced in very limited quantities. You need real stamina and smarts to be able to cover that much ground and still keep your head screwed on straight. The winery itself is a study in solidity, but not at the expense of an intimate quality. The Italianate main building, which houses the tasting room, winery, and cellars, is approached by steps that lead up to a thick oak door, bordered on either side by evergreen topiaries. As tasting rooms go, Wölffer's is fairly conservative, but visitors who gather here will be surrounded by lovely paintings by local artists, no shortage of dark wood, and they can study the rows of vines that march right up to the rear terrace. Vineyard manager Richard Pisacano keeps his acreage healthy, neat, and productive, as the estate's considerable output of wines, ranging from a steely Old World–style Chardonnay to a plummy, easygoing Merlot, indicates. Wölffer's wines, especially the relatively high-acid Chardonnays, also have a more decent record for aging than their North Fork competition, perhaps attributable to the slightly warmer microclimate of the South Fork. I've come across Wölffer Chards from the early 1990s that reminded me of a well-developed Chablis in their complexity and depth.

139 SAGG RD.
SAGAPONACK, NY 11962
631-537-5106
WWW.WOLFFER.COM

～◆ *LEFT:* Inspection of the fruit at Wölffer Estate ensures that grapes are unblem-
ished and perfectly ripe before they are crushed.

～◆ *RIGHT:* Though the Wölffer grounds were first used for training horses, not
making wine, they exude a pastoral tranquility.

CHANNING DAUGHTERS

If his neighbor Roman Roth is the most skilled winemaker on Long Island, then Larry Perrine of Channing Daughters is the most underrated. Why? Pride, if you ask me. Perrine refuses to take anything other than the long view when it comes to wine. Fortunately, Walter Channing—a wealthy businessman whose stark and fairly enormous sculptures, hewn from uprooted and inverted trees, cover the estate—has given Perrine plenty of room to maneuver. The result is a lineup of very serious, intelligently made wines that, in good vintages, really broadcast just how much potential the Long Island wine industry nurtures. Amateur stargazers will enjoy the nighttime sky-watcher weekends that the winery sponsors, in a field specially outfitted with structures to orient astronomers to the heavens.

1927 SCUTTLEHOLE RD.
BRIDGEHAMPTON, NY 11932
631-537-7224
WWW.CHANNINGDAUGHTERS.COM

DUCK WALK VINEYARDS

Duck Walk has been around for a while, but Dr. Herodotus Damianos' winery didn't pop onto a lot of people's radar until 2002, when it became embroiled in a lawsuit with a far better-known California winery. Dan Duckhorn, owner of Duckhorn Vineyards in Napa, decided that he could claim all rights to the word *duck* in a winery's name. Damianos disagreed, forcing Duckhorn to take him to court. The outcome remains unsettled, and the battle can be seen as symbolic of a larger East Coast–West Coast rivalry that is now emerging on the American wine landscape. But one thing's for sure: Duck Walk continues to produce a high-quality lineup of wines, from Chardonnay to Cabernet Sauvignon. This is among the most popular stops for wine tasting on the South Fork. It's situated on typically flat Long Island land, just off the Montauk Highway, a thoroughfare that's always jammed between Memorial and Labor Days.

231 MONTAUK HWY.
WATERMILL, NY 11976
631-726-7555
WWW.DUCKWALK.COM

SCHNEIDER VINEYARDS

Bruce Schneider and Christiane Baker Schneider are definitely a new breed. Rather than trying to produce competitive Long Island Merlot for which the available grape supply was already pretty slim, they focused on Cabernet Franc, an offbeat variety that was typically used to add aromatic complexity to Merlot-Cabernet blends. They have hit on something. Advised by the Premium Wine Group's Russell Hearn, an Australian, they created a rich, extracted wine of good complexity that captivated the palate of some wine critics. For a while they basically operated as *négociants,* a French tactic familiar to Burgundy lovers in which the guy who sells the wine doesn't actually own the vineyards but instead contracts with reputable growers for fruit. Keep an eye on Schneider. It could be pointing the way to North Fork's true future. The Schneiders have been planning to open their own winery for several years now, but for the moment you'll have to drop by a temporary location in Riverhead to see what they have to offer.

2248 ROANOKE AVE.
RIVERHEAD, NY
631-727-3334
WWW.SCHNEIDERVINEYARDS.COM

Coming out from under the shadow of its contested name, Duck Walk has proven that its expansive vineyards can produce great wines.

LABELS TO LOOK FOR

◎ BEDELL MAIN ROAD RED

A simple, straightforward red. An ideal wine to drink with hamburgers. A blend of Cabernet Sauvignon, Merlot, and Cabernet Franc.

◎ BEDELL C-BLOCK SOUTH MERLOT

Produced in small quantities, this rich, ageworthy Merlot is Bedell's best. Full-bodied but with outstanding complexity in good years.

◎ LENZ ESTATE SELECTION MERLOT

The biggest, richest Merlot on Long Island. Winemaker Eric Fry pulls out all the stops with this bottling.

◎ CHANNING DAUGHTERS "THE SCULPTOR" MERLOT

One of the most cultivated and carefully made Merlots on Long Island. Winemaker Larry Perrine has spent years perfecting this wine, which combines abundant fruit with outstanding structure and depth.

◎ RAPHAEL SAUVIGNON BLANC

Sauvignon Blanc isn't big on Long Island, but Raphael does a great job with this wine, which is released sooner than its oak-aged Merlots.

◎ RAPHAEL MERLOT

This is a fastidiously well-made wine, with all the fruit coming from Raphael's estate vineyards. Produced only in the best years, it shows Raphael's commitment to winemaking of the strictest quality.

☙ SCHNEIDER POTATO BARN RED

This is a lot of wine for the money ($15 a bottle). Produced from a cross section of Long Island's best red grapes—Merlot and Cabernet Franc—it spends sixteen months in oak, unusual for a wine at this price.

☙ SCHNEIDER CABERNET FRANC

At the moment, this is one of Long Island's best wines. If you want a taste of what the future of the region might be like, this is the wine you should sample. Aromatic, but also dripping with berry flavors.

☙ WÖLFFER ROSÉ

The ideal Long Island summer sipper. Perfect with seafood. Always sells out in a hurry.

☙ WÖLFFER ESTATE SELECTION CHARDONNAY

One of the few Long Island Chardonnays that actually has a track record for aging. That doesn't mean it can't be drunk right away, but it does have the structure to wait for a few years.

[AT A GLANCE: FINGER LAKES]

CENTRAL ROADS: Route 414 (East Seneca Lake); Route 14 (West Seneca Lake)

TOWNS TO VISIT: Watkins Glen, Elmira, Ithaca

LOCAL FLAVORS:
This is dairy country. Check out the local cheeses and,
of course, the famous Finger Lakes ice cream.

AVERAGE BOTTLE PRICE: $10

BEST TIME TO VISIT: May–October

WINERIES: Fifty-eight

ACRES OF VINES: 10,424

YEARLY WINE PRODUCTION: 25 million gallons

TOP WINES: Riesling, Cabernet Franc

WEBSITE: www.fingerlakeswinecountry.com

THE BOTTOM LINE:
The Finger Lakes is America's leading producer of high-quality Riesling.

CHAPTER *Two*

THE FINGER LAKES

Bully Hill slides down into Keuka Lake, one of the deep glacier-made lakes in the region.

AN INSPIRED RENAISSANCE

THE EMERGENCE OF LONG ISLAND in the 1970s did a lot to revive winemaking spirits in the Empire State. New York was back, baby.

Well, sort of. Since the midcentury, things had only gotten worse in the Hudson Valley. What had once been the heart and soul of New York winemaking and America's answer to the Loire Valley in France (according to *New York Times* food writers Matt and Ted Lee) was repositioning itself as a boutique agricultural region, perfecting everything *but* wine. By the late 1990s, you were far more likely to spot Hudson Valley foie gras on a restaurant menu than a Hudson Valley Pinot Noir on the wine list. Still, a few wineries were managing to bolster the region's cause. What they had going for them was magnificent scenery and lots and lots of small, picturesque towns neighboring the vineyards. If Long Island is trying to be New York's Napa, then the Hudson Valley is currently attempting to become the state's Sonoma.

Meanwhile, the slo-mo Finger Lakes, five hours north of New York City, adopted an antimarketing "We're Not Long Island," semistrategy that was beginning to pay off. A half-dozen wineries had decided to forget about aggressively pursuing that late twentieth-century winemaking Holy Grail—the boutique, critic-pleasing red—and instead dialed in on a grape variety that was a proven, if uneventful, regional performer: Riesling.

There was a time when German Riesling was regarded, in America, as superior to French red wine. In the 1960s and '70s, gooey domestic Riesling dominated the shelves in America's wine stores. People believed it was good stuff no matter how cloying it was and would drink it based on the shape of the bottle alone. By the 1990s, the California red-wine boom, not to mention dry Chardonnay, had pretty much knocked Riesling off its perch. It wasn't long before even the greatest German Rieslings were selling for what many wine

Though upstate New York is known for being chilly, the summer climate of the Finger Lakes allows for sunny days and boating, as well as grape-growing.

experts considered to be bargain-basement prices. The American version barely stood a chance in this market.

However, all was not lost. Riesling is a terrific grape in the vineyard: it goes and goes, rarely troubled by rotten weather or marginal climates. Why do you think it's reached its apotheosis in Germany, where the growing conditions are hardly competitive with, say, Tuscany's? But Riesling is also a naturally nuanced grape; it responds to where it is grown and can create, in the wine, an indelible stamp of origin. Chardonnay, except in Burgundy, can't do this. Nor can Sauvignon Blanc, or any of the other popular white grapes that these days dominate the dry-wine-drinking world.

HOW THE ICE AGE MADE GREAT WINE

Lo and behold, by the mid-'90s, a number of young Finger Lakes vintners had figured out that, in their region, they had something that even California didn't have: a strong sense of place. Sure, some California Cabernets showed terroir qualities. But Finger Lakes Rieslings had terroir to burn. These wines were undiscovered miracles of terroir, in fact. A small cadre of wine critics believed they were competitive with German Rieslings. The only other American wine state that had shown as much distinctiveness was Oregon, and its premium Pinot Noir business was booming.

The geography of the Finger Lakes couldn't be more different from New York's other two main regions. They're called *Finger Lakes* because they are extremely narrow, with dramatically sloping banks. The lakes themselves—cut by

[BASE CAMP]

The easiest way to get to the Finger Lakes is to fly into the Greater Rochester International Airport. But you can also go by rail (800-USA-RAIL) or bus (800-231-2222). If the low-key charm of the Finger Lakes wine country leaves you longing for a sophisticated respite, a night or two at **GENEVA ON THE LAKE** (1001 Lochland Rd., Geneva, 315-789-7190, above) should do the trick. If the Italianate architecture and formal gardens make you feel as though you've gotten in touch with your spiritual side, it might be because the place was once a monastery. Of course, a quiet bed-and-breakfast could be more to your taste; if so, check out the Finger Lakes Bed and Breakfast Association (www.flbba.com). Give **READING HOUSE** a try, where the breakfasts are out of this world, and be sure to ask proprietors Rita and Bill Newell to show you the Meadow Maze (4610 State Route 14, Rock Stream, 607-535-9785).

glaciers receding after the Ice Age—are deep, which means that they make excellent heat repositories during upstate New York's typically harsh winters. As it turns out, this is ideal Riesling country.

Fortunately, the winemakers had enough experience with top-notch Riesling to know what to go for: an expression of place, combined with ample fruit and scintillating acidic definition. There was no reason to mess around with barrels (Rieslings rarely see time in oak), so there wasn't much chance of messing up a good thing—or delaying its march to market. (Not that there has actually *been* a march to market yet, but there's hope.)

TURNING EXPECTATIONS ON THEIR HEAD

Ironically, then, in New York it's the most obscure and distant region that currently leads the never-ending quality quest. The state's classic region, the Hudson Valley, is struggling, while the hot new region, Long Island, might have gotten ahead of itself, putting marketing before quality in the bottle. Of course, all of the regions are physically glorious, far more varied than most other winemaking locales (with the possible exception of New Zealand and South Africa). There is also no shortage whatsoever of tasting rooms (unlike many at superpremium wineries in California).

In short, all three of New York's major winemaking regions cry out for visitors, and reward those who make the trip with astonishing overlooks of the Hudson River, vast blue skies above dramatic glacial lakes, and some of the

~~⌇⌇ Harvest time at Lamoreaux Landing.

finest views of the Atlantic to be had anywhere in America. All are also mercifully easy to deal with when compared with Napa Valley, with evolving services to handle the influx of tourists. (It's worth pointing out that the Flakes, as I like to call them, has achieved a level of excellence with Riesling that California can't hope to match—so it's not as if the Finger Lakes ever has to think of itself as being in direct competition with the wines of Mondavi and Gallo.)

There's something downright soothing about spending time in the Finger Lakes, where life really does seem to run according to the agricultural rhythms of a bygone era. And it isn't just the Amish and Mennonite dairy farmers, with their unhurried, no-tech ways, that give this part of the country its enchanted quality. The winemakers here have the chance to relax and develop their craft, while their counterparts in other regions are furiously competing against each other and international vintners. Yes, the Finger Lakes is old-fashioned and possibly too low-key for its own good, but then again, winemaking isn't a business that can be rushed, despite what the past few decades have wrought. Quality requires time.

Quality also requires financial stability. Perhaps the Finger Lakes' true secret weapon isn't modest expectations or stealthy expertise with an underrated grape. Rather, it's the great undiscussed requirement for superb wines: affordable vineyard land. This might be the only well-known, potentially great terroir in America where an aspiring winemaker can still afford to get in the game.

ROCHESTER

Keuka Lake

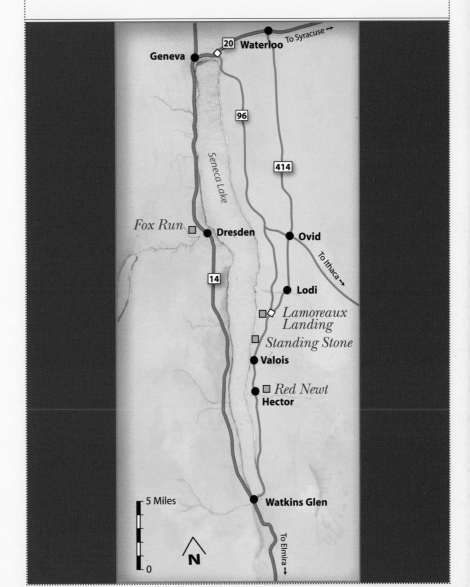

Geneva

20 Waterloo

To Syracuse →

96

414

Fox Run Dresden

Ovid

To Ithaca →

14

Lodi

Lamoreaux Landing

Standing Stone

Valois

Red Newt

Hector

Seneca Lake

5 Miles

Watkins Glen

To Elmira →

N

0

Fox Run Vineyards, on the shores of Lake Seneca, hosts an annual garlic festival where visitors can pair their wines with gourmet garlic-themed dishes.

~~⌘ Fox Run's café, where sandwiches and salads are available to balance out a rigorous tasting.

FOX RUN VINEYARDS

Fox Run (and yes, there are foxes about) is one of the most technologically advanced and contemporary looking of the new generation of wineries. Its Cabernet Franc is its best wine, but its Pinot Noir is coming along nicely, as are its Riesling and Chardonnay. The tasting room is an airy, open space where you can also obtain a delicious lunch, compliments of Fox Run's in-house café. The winemaking operation is housed nearby in a prefab structure. Fox Run is a true regional leader; if you visit only one Finger Lakes winery, this should be the one. Everything that's good about the region in encapsulated in the winery's philosophy, which is to combine quality with broadened distribution. If you're lucky, owner Scott Osborn will be around to fill you in on why the Finger Lakes should be America's answer to Germany's Mosel. Osborn cut his teeth in California before returning to his native Finger Lakes. He is probably the least provincial guy in a winemaking region that has, in the past, suffered no shortage of provincialism. The man has a plan. His goal is to increase the supply of top-caliber grapes by expanding vineyard plantings, especially in Riesling. He also hopes that Finger Lakes' vintners can enhance their overall wine quality, boosting

670 ROUTE 14
PENN YAN, NY 14527
800-636-9786
WWW.FOXRUNVINEYARDS.COM

their best wines into a clearly premium category, thus securing a better price per bottle, and thus securing more capital to invest in marketing. If the Finger Lakes has a leader, Osborn is it.

LAMOREAUX LANDING WINE CELLARS

Easily the Finger Lakes' most architecturally dramatic winery, Lamoreaux merges elements of classic upstate New York barn architecture with owner Mark Wagner's ideas about Greek temples. The result is a soaring Greek Revival structure that affords stunning views of Seneca Lake but still functions as a working winery (barrels are stacked high rather than laid out, due to the cellar's small footprint). Wagner is a Pinot Noir enthusiast—many in the Finger Lakes are, citing the cooler growing climate—but Lamoreaux's portfolio of wines also includes Chardonnay, Gewürztraminer, and sparkling wines. Nearby Cornell University is making a claim to become the East's equivalent of the University of California at Davis, the nation's preeminent center for wine research and education. Cornell has established several vineyards on the Lamoreaux property to experiment with different types of grapes.

9224 ROUTE 414
LODI, NEW YORK 14860
607-582-6011
WWW.LAMOREAUXWINE.COM

LEFT: Lamoreaux Landing's well-tended vineyards, which are overseen by owner Mark Wagner.

The grounds of Lamoreaux Landing's winery are surrounded by miles of farmland and have an excellent view of Lake Seneca.

The Standing Stone vineyard's name comes from the Dutch name for the local Native American tribe, the Seneca.

STANDING STONE VINEYARDS

Along with Red Newt, Standing Stone is a quality leader in the Finger Lakes region. Owners Tom and Marti Macinski are, to put it mildly, winging it (as much as you can wing it, having been in business since 1991). Although they come off as a slightly zany couple, making up their wines as they go along, they have pioneered the Finger Lakes' new focus on premium Riesling. They also market their wines better than most of their neighbors. Marti handles the bulk of the winemaking duties, while Tom keeps track of the finances. Their winery is a borderline shabby affair, a pale green and yellow edifice that all but sinks into the landscape. Their vineyards are full of weeds, but their Riesling and Gewürztraminer are out of this world. It goes to show you that talent and dedication can sometimes make up for a lack of experience. What distinguishes the Macinskis from the competition is their commitment to getting their wines into the nearest major Finger Lakes market, New York City. Given the generally very high quality of Finger Lakes whites, it's frankly astonishing that they aren't better exposed in Manhattan. Chalk it up to ingrained resistance. New Yorkers, if they're even aware of the Finger Lakes at all, think of it as a sleepy realm of farmers, not as a viable alternative to Napa Valley. As Tom and Marti develop their brand, keep and eye out for their superb wines. Like the formally unappreciated New Zealand Sauvignon Blancs already have, their Gewürz and Riesling are bound to command higher prices in years to come. Standing Stone is absolutely worth a visit, especially if you both want to catch a rising star and enjoy seeing what pluck, ambition, and hard work can accomplish.

9934 ROUTE 414
HECTOR, NY 14841
800-803-7135
WWW.STANDINGSTONEWINES.COM

On the deck of the tasting room, Standing Stone's Smokehouse Café serves an array of cheeses to go with its wines.

Red Newt has been operating for only five years, but it already produces a number of different red and white wines.

RED NEWT CELLARS

Dave Whiting is the Finger Lakes' best winemaker. It shows especially in his Rieslings, which can challenge those from Germany and Alsace for quality. With Standing Stone, Red Newt (named for the small, lizard-like creatures that live in the vineyard) has thus far produced the only Finger Lakes white that truly suggests strong aging potential. This is a result of two things: intelligent grape sourcing and local knowledge. Whiting knows his way around the region, having labored here for decades (he was briefly involved with Standing Stone, before the Macinskis went it alone). Red Newt's winemaking facility is no-nonsense, and the tasting room, while substantial, really plays second fiddle to the winery's bistro, where Dave's wife, Debra, helms the stoves. The winery building itself is a modern affair, a simple, dark, wooden shape with a decorative vineyard out front. From the deck, the views of Seneca Lake are extraordinary, a deeply pleasing place to eat an early dinner and sample a taste or two of the Finger Lakes' boundless future. The Whitings don't have aggressive plans for expansion, but in the end, that could be a good thing, as Tom's skills and devotion to taking it slow could lead to a Finger Lakes wine that finally achieves breakout national attention.

3675 TICHENOR RD.
HECTOR, NY 14841
607-546-4100
WWW.REDNEWT.COM

The menu at Red Newt's Bistro is extensive, and the summer seating on the deck makes for memorable views and meals.

*L*ABELS TO LOOK FOR

🌀 FOX RUN DRY RIESLING

Dry of course means "not as sweet as you're used to from New York Riesling." An excellent introduction to the Finger Lakes' signature varietal.

🌀 FOX RUN CABERNET FRANC

Probably Fox Run's best wine, and a good indication of what this lighter-weight red can do in the region.

🌀 RED NEWT RIESLING DRY RESERVE

The Finger Lakes' best wine. This Riesling is competitive with versions from France and Germany. Absolutely delicious, complex, and with solid aging potential. The Finger Lakes' distinctive terroir really comes through.

🌀 RED NEWT RIESLING SEMI-DRY

A touch sweeter than the Riesling Dry Reserve, this is less expensive and nonetheless a winner for the region.

🌀 STANDING STONE RIESLING

This is the Finger Lakes' second-best Riesling, right behind Red Newt's Dry Reserve. Also loaded with Finger Lakes terroir.

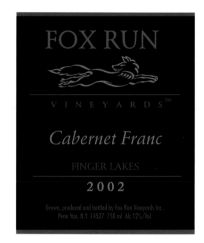

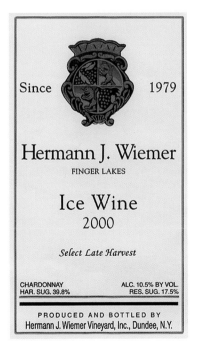

STANDING STONE GEWÜRTZTRAMINER
Riesling is great in the Finger Lakes, but so is this other white varietal. Standing Stone's is rich and spicy and not at all sticky sweet.

LAMOREAUX LANDING DRY RIESLING
Another wonderful Finger Lakes Riesling—and from a winery that tends to focus more heavily on Chardonnay as its principal white.

LAMOREAUX LANDING PINOT NOIR
Finger Lakes winemakers are somewhat preoccupied with Pinot Noir as their potential breakout red wine. Success with the finicky grape hasn't been stupendous, but this one shows potential. Lots of nice cherry flavors.

HERMANN J. WIEMER DRY JOHANNISBERG RIESLING RESERVE
Wiemer has long been a Finger Lakes stalwart, making sure that the region garners national attention. This wine is a bit old-fashioned but still a fine example of the region's signature grape.

HERMANN J. WIEMER SELECT LATE HARVEST ICE WINE
Because it can get pretty cold toward the end of the harvest in the Finger Lakes, it's possible to produce an ice wine, a wine made from grapes that have frozen on the vine. The result is a rich, sweet, dessert wine.

[AT A GLANCE: PENNSYLVANIA]

CENTRAL ROAD: Route 1

TOWNS TO VISIT:
Chadds Ford, New Hope, York.

LOCAL FLAVORS:
New Jersey tomatoes are well known and highly coveted; they reach their apotheosis in August. Look for farm stands and farmers' markets. The blueberries aren't bad, either.

AVERAGE BOTTLE PRICE: $10–15

BEST TIME TO VISIT: April–October

WINERIES: Seventy-plus

ACRES OF VINES: 14,000

YEARLY WINE PRODUCTION:
500,000 gallons

TOP WINES: Chardonnay, Riesling

WEBSITE: www.pennsylvaniawines.com

THE BOTTOM LINE:
Pennsylvania has taken the lead for Chardonnay production in the mid-Atlantic.

CHAPTER *Three*

THE
MID-ATLANTIC

DOWN TO EARTH

LET'S FACE IT: When it comes to the mid-Atlantic region—loosely defined as everything south of New York and north of Maryland and Virginia—what do people most often think of? Interstate 1-95? The Jersey Turnpike? The *Pennsylvania* Turnpike? Amish country? Cows? Heavy industry? The City of Brotherly Love? *The Sopranos*? Wine is probably the last thing people think of.

Well, surprise surprise! They should change their thinking. Not only do New Jersey and Pennsylvania cover a lot of geographical—much of it idyllic, rolling farmland—but these states also boast wine industries. Wine industries, incidentally, that have been around for a while. And wine industries that are thriving.

Now, it's true that *any* regional wine scene—outside California, Oregon, Washington, and (to an increasing extent) New York's Long Island—is going to be a little bit hokey. Big deal! Not everybody wants to visit wine country in places where celebrities are endlessly buzzing the vineyards in Gulfstream V private jets, where droves of tourists are clogging the roads in stretch Hummer limos, and where most, if not all, of the winery tasting rooms charge $5 for a one-ounce pour of an alleged elixir that wine critic Robert M. Parker, Jr. scored eighty-seven points.

New Jersey and especially Pennsylvania are also perfect for the sort of adventurous oenophile who wants to get slightly off the grid but doesn't want to have to head off to Slovenia or South Africa. Ideal, in other words, for the viticulturally curious who are happy to explore their own backyards. The best thing about mid-Atlantic wine country is the sheer sincerity of it all. It's almost like wine here is treated as if it were still a basic agricultural product, not some sort of highfalutin expression of a snob culture. All very 4-H. Enchantingly Mayberry. But not—and I stress *not*—bumpkin-ish. Wine naturally prevents those who pro-

〜⧽ The grape juice vineyards in North East, Pennsylvania, with the Mercyhurst College campus behind.

THE BRANDYWINE RIVER MUSEUM (U. S. Route 1, 610-388-2700, above) features an extensive collection of works by the Wyeth family, perhaps the best-known clan of American painters. For Civil War buffs, **GETTYSBURG** isn't too far away from the Brandywine Valley. Every American owes it to himself or herself to visit the National Park, which is adorned with numerous monuments. Revolutionary War buffs can visit the **BRANDY-WINE BATTLEFIELD PARK** (1491 Baltimore Pike, Chadds Ford, 610-459-3342), where Americans battled the British in 1777. When in Jersey, do as Jerseyites do: Head to Atlantic City and check out the **BORGATA**, a new casino and resort with one of the finest wine programs on the East Coast (1 Borgata Way, 866-692-6742).

duce it from becoming, or remaining, rubes, if only because they have to be at least peripherally aware of the great winemaking traditions of Europe. This can lead to some amusingly disorienting conversation. You drive around the Jersey countryside, you find a cute little winery, and, expecting not a whole lot, you drop in, only to find yourself half an hour later engrossed in a discussion of vintages in Burgundy dating back to the 1970s.

UNDER THE RADAR

That's what makes this region even more charming: the seriousness with which the winemakers regard their craft within their own circles. No, you're not likely to encounter a whole lot of scores for Pennsylvania Chardonnays in the pages of *Wine Spectator* or the *Wine Advocate*. But if you pay attention to winery Web sites, checking in now and then you'll discover that mid-Atlantic vintners are constantly submitting their wines to state-fair-type competitions. You have to take medals and ribbons with a grain of salt, in the wine world anyway. But winemakers in New Jersey and Pennsylvania are certainly proud enough to tell *absolutely anyone who will listen* that they were awarded the gold medal for their Proprietor's Red, silver for their Blackberry Spumanté, or bronze for their Cabernet Sauvignon at the most recent farm show.

Like every other winemaking region in America—that isn't on the West Coast—the mid-Atlantic has gone through substantial changes as the wine boom of the 1980s and '90s redefined viticulture in this country. "Quality wines" are now almost universally defined as those made

The vineyards of Naylor Wine Cellars in Stewartstown, Pennsylvania, which makes more than two dozen kinds of wine.

from vinifera grapes. We're talking Merlot, Cabernet Sauvignon, Chardonnay and so on here—European varieties—not the native varieties and French hybrids, as well as the fruit wines that formerly characterized much of America's regional scene.

Every regional wine producer who wants to be taken seriously has made the switch. Which is not to say that they don't keep a few good-selling legacy wines around the tasting room; of course they do. But increasingly they are staking their futures on the grapes and the wines that have succeeded at the international level and that are regarded by critics and successful winemakers as producing the best wines. Currently, there are seventy wineries in Pennsylvania alone; at least a few of them *have* to be aiming for a certain amount of national attention. And the best way to do that is to focus wines made from the same grapes that have shown their mettle in California (not to mention in Europe, for the past few centuries).

A KEYSTONE IDYLL

Pennsylvania's wine country consists of seven major regions: Lake Erie; Pittsburgh Countryside; Groundhog Region; Upper Susquehanna; Lower Susquehanna; Lehigh Valley and Berks County; and Philly Countryside. These are not all official AVAs, as recognized by the U.S. Treasury Department's Bureau of Alcohol, Tobacco, and Firearms. One that is, the Lake Erie AVA, is shared with Ohio. (AVA status, by the way, is important for a regional winery, because it means you're on the U.S. government's map.)

New Jersey's wineries are spread throughout the state and are grouped by the Garden State Wine Growers Association (www.newjerseywines.com) into three regions, none of which have AVA status: North, South, and Middle.

Altogether, Pennsylvania has around three times as many wineries as New Jersey and by far the more organized structure of wine trails. Conveniently, however, you can make a day (or a few days) out of a Pennsylvania–New Jersey sojourn by driving back and forth across the Delaware River, visiting wineries on either side. In fact, the river is one of the major geographical features that serve to buffer the region's climate from harsher weather coming from the Atlantic. If you've never spent any time in this part of the country—and if your preconceptions of both states are limited to the aforementioned industrial clichés—you're in for a treat, especially if you like to drive. This countryside is truly some of the most beautiful anywhere—rolling and lush and green, adorned with small farms and quaint towns. Perhaps as picturesque as the Delaware River is the area's western natural border, the blue hills of the Allegheny Mountains. This is the countryside that inspired the great American painter Andrew Wyeth. It's also an area steeped in history. When the old man himself, William Penn, settled here, the countryside reminded him of France, and so he started growing vines in 1684. In 1793, the new nation had its first winery, the Pennsylvania Wine Company. So get a map and start marching. Trust me, the mid-Atlantic region is anything but middling when it comes to wine.

Getting to the Brandywine Valley is easy: Philadelphia International Airport is within minutes of the wine country. Visitors to the Brandywine Valley will want to check out a list of charming B&Bs in operation in this historic region (www.thebrandywine.com). **SEVEN SPRINGS MOUNTAIN RESORT** (777 Waterwheel Drive, Champion, 800-452-2223, above) hosts an annual wine and food festival. Once you've eaten your fill and sampled plenty of wine, you can unwind with a concert, or hit the links for a round of golf. **THE BRANDYWINE RIVER HOTEL** (1609 Baltimore Pike, Chadds Ford, 800-274-9644) is a feast for lovers of antique charm.

Owner John Crouch tends to vines at Allegro Vineyards, founded by Crouch and his brother, in Brogue, Pennsylvania.

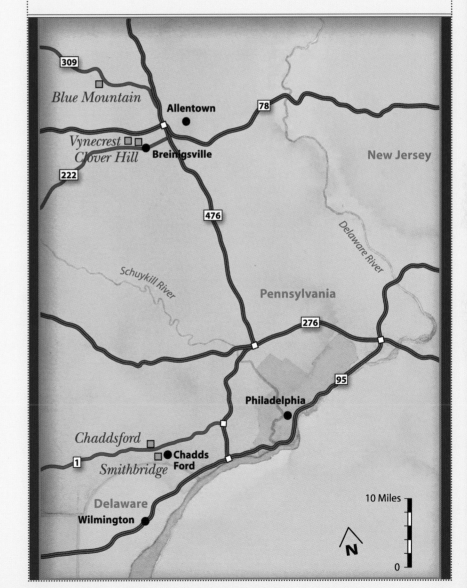

PHILADELPHIA

309

Blue Mountain

Allentown

78

New Jersey

Vynecrest
Clover Hill   Breinigsville

222

476

Delaware River

Pennsylvania

Schuykill River

276

95

Philadelphia

Chaddsford

1   Chadds Ford
Smithbridge

Delaware

Wilmington

10 Miles

N

0

CHADDSFORD WINERY

Chaddsford is the most successful winery in Pennsylvania in terms of national attention. The wines produced here are routinely cited by national media as leaders in the entire U.S. regional wine scene, not just in the mid-Atlantic area. The winemaker, Eric Miller, has an interesting connection to another regional pioneer, the Benmarl winery in New York's Hudson Valley: Benmarl is owned and operated by his father, Mark Miller, a man who was instrumental in bringing the Burgundian gospel of premium winemaking, based on terroir, to America in the 1960s. In Burgundy, the only white grape permitted is Chardonnay. As it turns out, Eric has become particularly devoted to Chardonnay. He must have gauged his terroir well: Chaddsford's Chards tend to consistently garner accolades. Eric has transferred what he learned at Benmarl to the Pennsylvania countryside but as one might expect, has adapted a winemaking philosophy with a more modern perspective than his father's. His skill is evident in his various Chardonnay bottlings, as well as his Pinot Noir and a Bordeaux-style red blend called Merican. Grapes come from Chaddsford's own 19-acre vineyard as well as many other area growers. The winery itself—housed in a restored eighteenth-century barn decorated with antiques—is a touchstone for the entire region, offering an extensive schedule of food-and-wine related events during the year, as well as concerts and cultural performances.

632 BALTIMORE PIKE
CHADDS FORD, PA 19317
610-388-6221
WWW.CHADDSFORD.COM

ABOVE LEFT: Rows of vines at Chaddsford.

ABOVE RIGHT: The Miller residence on the grounds of the Chaddsford Winery.

OPPOSITE: Chaddsford's renovated barn, which began serving as a winery in 1982.

BLUE MOUNTAIN VINEYARDS

The proprietors, Joe and Vickie Greff, established this home-grown winery in 1986, on the shores of several ponds, with views of the Blue Ridge Mountains, in typical Pennsylvania-regional fashion. They did what a lot of regional winemakers do with their first five acres: They planted hardy grape varieties that almost no one who drinks wine has ever heard of. Chambourcin, Vignoles, and Vidal Blanc, to name three that don't exactly ring in your ears the same way that, oh, say, Merlot, Chardonnay, and Cabernet Sauvignon do. Fortunately, they didn't stick with these French hybrid grapes. Instead, as they expanded, they put in more vinifera vines and joined a trend in regional American winemaking. Now, almost twenty years later, they have nearly one hundred acres of Chardonnay, Riesling, Pinot Noir, Cabernet Franc, Cabernet Sauvignon, and Syrah, among other well-regarded international varieties. Their wines have gained strong attention from the national press—including *USA Today*—which also reported on what Joe and Vickie were doing before they caught the wine bug: growing Christmas trees. Old St. Nick's loss is the Pennsylvania wine industry's gain. Their Blue Heron Meritage is proof that Pennsylvania can produce superb European-style red blends. The winery itself is reminiscent of the kind of place you find in Mendocino County, in California: rustic and inviting.

7627 GRAPE VINE DR.

NEW TRIPOLI, PA 18066

610-298-3068

WWW.BLUEMOUNTAINWINE.COM

 Blue Mountain Vineyards, where two historic buildings will be restored and included on the National Register of Historic Places. Though the historic areas are not open to visitors yet, the winery itself includes ponds and an outdoor terrace.

CLOVER HILL VINEYARDS AND WINERY

9850 NEWTOWN RD.
BREINIGSVILLE, PA 18031
1-888-CLOVERHILL
WWW.CLOVERHILLWINERY.COM

Many regional wineries seem to consist primarily of a tasting room with a small garage attached, which is where the wine is made. Clover Hill is a different story. There's one of these wineries in every region: a place that's technically state of the art. In Clover Hill's case, the facility is hard to miss: a cluster of low-slung red buildings stands out amid the surrounding vines and green farm country. In 2002, the winery rolled out plans for further expansion. Wine production here, under the supervision of winemaker John Skrip III, ranges across a fairly broad spectrum (as one might expect, given a yearly case production of nineteen thousand cases). My advice is to focus on his "Generations" bottlings, a Chardonnay and a Riesling that provide a strong sense of what the winery is capable of. The wines are called "Generations," by the way, because there are currently three generations of Skrips involved in the family business.

Grapes grown on the Clover Hill Vineyards property.

John Skrip III is typical of the new generation of regional American winemakers. His parents, John and Pat Skrip II, opened Clover Hill Vineyards and Winery in the mid-1980s, just as the wine-country lifestyle was beginning to become alluring for many people living in states outside California. Raising children in the business effectively established a sort of succession plan, one that John III has seized on. But unlike his parents, John III has received specialized training in enology—in California, no less, at California State University in Fresno—something that big winemaking regions consider to be de rigueur for even apprentice vintners. Now, he possesses both the on-the-job experience and the professional expertise to lead the country's fourth-largest wine-producing state to the next level. And Clover Hill's high-caliber winemaking facility certainly helps.

Vynecrest's vineyards in the snow (left) and mist (right); the vines here can endure all kinds of Pennsylvania weather, allowing the winery to use only estate-grown grapes in its wines.

VYNECREST WINERY

The big selling point at Vynecrest is the fact that all their wines are made from estate-grown grapes. This might not sound like much—in fact, it might sound obvious—but it's shocking how many regional American wineries truck grape juice in from superior growing areas (i.e., California) and then pass the resulting wines off as entirely their own. Vynecrest doesn't play that game. Housed in a restored nineteenth-century barn, Vynecrest offers a fairly typical Pennsylvania regional lineup of wines. Give the Seyval Blanc, the Traminette, or the Cabernet Franc a shot. These are all wines that have the potential to move Pennsylvania's winemaking to the next level. Vynecrest deserves a lot of credit for committing to the offbeat varietals.

172 ARROWHEAD LN.
BREINIGSVILLE, PA 18031
800-361-0725
WWW.VYNECREST.COM

SMITHBRIDGE CELLARS

If not the most serious winery in Pennsylvania, then certainly a candidate. Perhaps the *strongest* candidate. Anyway, there aren't too many American regional wineries that proclaim the complete commitment to vinifera grapes as loudly as Smithbridge. It's commendable, given Pennsylvania's at-times fairly harsh climate. Personally, I adore this philosophy; in Virginia, just a few vintners with this level of devotion to vinifera grapes have put that state in the national limelight. Smithbridge's approach could do the same for Pennsylvania and the Brandywine Valley. Of particular interest here are the Chardonnay and the Hearthstone Meritage red blend. The winery itself is a lovely, rustic, laid-back affair: not much more than a stone-and-shingle barn. It's one of the many ways this classy operation identifies with its Old World spiritual guide, Burgundy.

159 BEAVER VALLEY RD.

CHADDS FORD, PA 19317

610-558-4703

WWW.SMITHBRIDGE.COM

ℒABELS TO LOOK FOR

ⓒ CHADDSFORD PHILIP ROTH VINEYARD CHARDONNAY

Eric Miller's premier Chardonnay, and his calling card to the wider wine world. Produced in the Burgundian *terroir* style, with lots of complexity underlying rich fruit flavors. (Terroir, by the way, means that the unique flavors of geography—the taste of the soil, if you will, mysteriously get into the wine.)

ⓒ CHADDSFORD MILLER ESTATE VINEYARD CHARDONNAY

Produced only from estate-grown fruit, this is a bit less expensive than the Philip Roth Vineyard bottling but no less compelling.

ⓒ CHADDSFORD CABERNET/CHAMBOURCIN

Chambourcin is one of those grape varieties that isn't often heard of these days. It's a French-hybrid grape that has been around only since the early 1960s. It's fairly full-bodied, if unsophisticated, and it does well in humid climates. At Chaddsford, it's blended with the more pedigreed Cabernet Sauvignon, yielding a robust red.

ⓒ BLUE MOUNTAIN VINEYARDS BLUE HERON MERITAGE

A classic Bordeaux blend of Cabernet Sauvignon, Merlot, and Cabernet Franc, this red is also aged in French-oak barrels. One of Pennsylvania's more serious wines.

ⓒ BLUE MOUNTAIN ICE WINE

One of the ways in which Pennsylvania winemakers can use hybrid-grape varieties such as Vidal Blanc is in ice wines, where their less-attractive qualities can be overcome by the incredible concentration

that allowing grapes to freeze on the vine can provide. Grapes for this ice wine are harvested in February.

☙ CLOVER HILL GENERATIONS CHARDONNAY
According to winemaker John Skrip III, the goal with this all-estate-grown Chardonnay was to impress colleagues from his California days. This Chard has one of the best quality-to-price ratios of any wine produced in Pennsylvania.

☙ CLOVER HILL GENERATIONS RIESLING
A lot of mid-Atlantic winemakers resist Riesling because they think it will be tough to sell. However, the smart ones know that Riesling has one of the longest track records for excellence of any wine. Many younger winemakers prefer Rieslings in a dry style, and that's just what John Skrip III's daughter, Kari Skrip, has created here.

☙ SMITHBRIDGE CELLARS SWEET RIESLING
Late-harvest dessert-style wines are often a safe bet. Riesling can do particularly well in this style, as consumers are already accustomed to drinking it on the sweet side. (Plus, American winemakers have lots of experience with it, and it doesn't make too much trouble, unlike a dicey grape, such as the Pinot Noir.) This one is a great deal.

☙ VYNECREST RIESLING
Reisling is often a tourist's best introduction to regional wines, and this version is no exception.

[AT A GLANCE: VIRGINIA]

CENTRAL ROADS: Highways 81, 64, and 66.

TOWNS TO VISIT:
Don't miss Charlottesville, the town that Thomas Jefferson built.
The University of Virginia and Jefferson's estate, Monticello, are both
magnificent. Northern Virginia provides easy access to Washington, D. C.

LOCAL FLAVORS:
Just about everyone has heard of Virginia ham,
but the state also produces great apples and peanuts.
North Carolina barbecue is unique.

AVERAGE BOTTLE PRICE: $10–15

BEST TIME TO VISIT: March–November

WINERIES: Eighty-plus

ACRES OF VINES: 2,250

YEARLY WINE PRODUCTION: 680,000 gallons

TOP WINES: Cabernet Sauvignon, Syrah, Chardonnay, Viognier

WEBSITE: www.virginiawines.com

THE BOTTOM LINE:
The state has become the Southeast's quality leader.

CHAPTER Four

THE SOUTHEAST

THOMAS JEFFERSON'S DREAM

THERE'S A TRAIN LEAVING THE STATION in American regional winemaking, and the U.S. Southeast is pulling it. In fact, since the early 1990s, states such as Virginia and North Carolina have much more firmly established themselves as the locomotive.

Now, we're not talking about a coast-to-coast flyer here. On the whole, the southeastern wine industry is underpowered by comparison with California, Oregon, and Washington. But there's no shortage of intelligence being applied to winemaking in this neck of the woods. Virginia's most famous vintner, Thomas Jefferson (who never really managed to get the Old Dominion's eighteenth-century wine revolution off the ground), would be proud.

Let's do some comparisons. In California, you can find American winemaking in its most diverse and successful form. You've got your inexpensive megaproducers and your vast vineyards, but also lots of in-between premium producers and certainly a goodly number of superpremium— and even double super-premium—operations. You name it, its there in the Golden State.

Washington and Oregon have adopted a very different model. Both have decided to concentrate exclusively on premium wines. No jug wines, no plonk, no cheap rotgut. The market share they want to grab is at the highly profitable upper end.

Texas is trying to make the California model work: a mixture of premium and subpremium wines, across a wide variety of grape types and wine styles. The Southeast, by and large, is aiming to emulate Oregon. (And just to follow the argument, Pennsylvania is looking to New York for inspiration, seeking to copy the Empire State's profitable tasting-room approach; while midwestern wineries are still

The fields of Barboursville Vineyards in Virginia.

If you're in the neighborhood of central Virginia, you should consider spending a few hours touring the campus of the **UNIVERSITY OF VIRGINIA** (Charlottesville, 434-924-0311), then heading over to check out founder and third U.S. president—and America's first oenophile—Thomas Jefferson's residence, **MONTICELLO** (980 Thomas Jefferson Parkway, 434-984-9844, above). The entire Jeffersonian vision is a study in American neoclassical architecture at its very best. **COLONIAL WILLIAMSBURG**, between Richmond and Norfolk, has long been a favorite of historically-minded vacationing families. Golfers will want to consider an excursion to White Sulphur Springs, and the famous **GREENBRIER RESORT** (300 West Main St., White Sulphur Springs, WV, 800-453-4858).

in the process of ramping up their grape supply and their winemaking skills.)

THE SOUTH SHALL RISE TO THE CHALLENGE

You never know what's going to work, but given that the *international* wine scene is becoming much more competitive, the Oregon model seems better than the California one. And it pleases me to see Virginia, with its long history with the vine, leading the way in the Southeast.

There is a small problem, however: Virginia wine country is spread out all over the state. There are worthy producers in the northern corner, up by Washington, D. C., in the middle, and in the southern part of the state. My feeling is that this has created a sort of regionalism within the region, preventing Virginia's winemakers from clearly establishing their state's signature wine. The vintners here communicate with each other, but their growing conditions are so variegated—terraced mountain vineyards here, flat expanses there—that what works quite well in one place fails utterly in another. Then there's the climate, which is hardly Mediterranean (summers are remorselessly humid). This means that disease is an ever-present threat, as is too much rain during the harvest.

Challenging? You bet. By contrast, Californians have it blissfully easy. And Virginia's vintners will tell you that as a sly means of lauding their own talents as *winemakers*

The back side of the Biltmore House, the largest privately owned home in the country, which includes an indoor pool, bowling alley, and 250 rooms.

[OLD-SCHOOL FARMING]

SUSTAINABLE AGRICULTURE

"Sustainability" has become a preoccupation of many American regional winemakers. Sustainable agriculture is not really new—it dates at least to the broad organic agriculture movements of the 1960s (and could even be dated in America back to Thomas Jefferson)—but it is a somewhat fresh experience for winemakers, who have traditionally used at least a small quantity of pesticides and fertilizers to control vineyard disease and encourage healthy vine development. Some regional winemakers have made sustainability a selling point for their wines, eschewing all methods of modern farming, favoring instead an approach that allows their grapes to develop with minimal intervention, beyond basic pruning. A few even disdain sulfites, which are often added to wines late in the game to stabilize them before bottling. These wines are generally labeled as "organic." Other advocates of sustainability merely look for ways in which they can treat their vineyards more gently, preserving them for later generations. Some big players have come around to this point of view, including Robert Mondavi in Napa and most of the important winemakers in Oregon. Some of sustainable agriculture's broader themes have not been widely adopted by winemakers. For example, the notion that food should be cultivated in ways that are economically just on a global scale doesn't apply to wine, because it is after all a luxury beverage (at least to most people). Other aspects of sustainability have always been part of the winemaker's creed because vintners invariably hope to maintain the health of their vineyards for future generations. Nowadays, they strive to maintain an equilibrium between their vineyards and their surrounding environments (Sam Sebastiani's California winery is situated near a wetland). They aren't always successful—birds can be a problem for grapes—but they have certainly made the effort. The results are frequently seen in the bottle: wines that are minimally "treated" tend to be superior to wines that have been elaborately "manipulated," and most winemakers will tell you that quality can invariably be traced to the vineyard.

rather than grape growers. They often have to make more from less. They also have to aim for a style that is altogether less full and robust—less automatic—than many California wines possess. Naturally, they take their cues from Europe, rather than the West Coast.

Of course, this doesn't mean they can't fantasize. Chardonnay is the most planted grape in the state, and many Virginia vintners would dearly love to bring out a truly killer Blue Ridge Chardonnay or Cabernet Sauvignon. But this is unlikely. And a number of folks have figured it out. So they are concentrating on Rhône-style varietals, such as Viognier and Syrah. This is smart. Both these wines are currently hip. It's far easier to build a little buzz with them than to enter the competitive fray with yet another Chard.

Virginia's wine trails are eminently worth seeking out. The country is truly beautiful, with an abundance of picturesque back roads that twist and wind among horse farms, fruit orchards, through college towns, and in and out of hilly locales adorned with charming barns and unpretentious country houses. This is the land of the old aristocratic tradition of the foxhunt, and numerous riding clubs make for classic spectator events. (Bring or rent a car that handles well—this is some of the best driving country this side of Sonoma. The famed Skyline Drive that winds through the Blue Ridge Mountains to the west is not to be missed.) If you visit in early October, you can catch the Monticello Wine Festival.

Elsewhere in the Southeast, both North Carolina and Georgia have managed to produce wines of surprisingly good quality. The trouble spots are where you might imagine them to be: Florida, Louisiana, and other areas closer to the tropics. There are wineries in America's more torpid regions, but their wines are not going to make anyone want to give up Napa Chardonnay in order to drink local anytime soon.

Of particular interest in North Carolina is the Yadkin Valley, the state's first AVA, located between Winston-Salem and Asheville. There are seven wineries clustered here in the northeast corner of the state (overall, North Carolina has more than thirty wineries). It makes sense that this region would support good winemaking in the Tar Heel State: Temperatures here tend to be substantially cooler than in other parts of the state, due to the altitude of the Blue Ridge Mountains. This piedmont country, home to the real small-town model for Mayberry and some superb barbecue, has long been the state's produce center. This area is magnificent for everything, from driving to hiking to biking. A company called Discover Adventures currently offers several package tours of the region that range into northern Georgia. Most wineries in North Carolina feature a mix of vinifera wines and wines made from native varietals. Many also operate tasting rooms, open to the public for the majority of the year.

~~⦵ The ruins of the Barbour mansion, designed by Thomas Jefferson for James Barbour, who served as Virginia's Governor and Senator, Defense Secretary under John Quincy Adams, and Ambassador to Great Britain. The house was destroyed by fire on Christmas Day, 1884.

VIRGINIA

LINDEN VINEYARDS

A little slice of heaven in northern Virginia, Linden is a bit tricky to find—it's back roads all the way—but once there, you might not want to leave. The winery and tasting room are combined in a simple, unpretentious building that blends beautifully into the hilly landscape. It's staffed by eager young people who can't wait to share winemaker Jim Law's philosophy of the vine. Law himself is a key Virginia winemaking personality. A mellow, easygoing, but sill intense guy, he's happiest when he's making wine or greeting visitors. Marketing isn't his thing. As a result, Linden Vineyards' wines perhaps haven't received as much exposure as they should. But Law doesn't care; he's content to walk his estate in near-perfect tranquility, the embodiment of Thomas Jefferson's American ideal. It's easy to understand why he's so delighted to be here. Linden is beautiful. You drive past Law's house, then past the apple orchard before reaching the winery and tasting room atop a hill. Vineyards roll away in every direction; the grapevines are trellised in numerous ways, showcasing Law's appetite for experimentation. Law can be a little prickly about how the winery is used. He lives here, after all, so the place shuts down at five each evening (and is only open from Wednesday to Sunday, during the season). Large groups are spurned, and although Linden sells artisanal foods (sausages and cheeses), it doesn't have a restaurant on site. Picnics and contemplation, from the winery's deck, are encouraged; parties are not. Tours of the winery are conducted (as long as you let them know you're interested), and periodically during the year Law conducts winemaking seminars.

Law represents almost literally the soul of Virginia winemaking. Travel from one end of the state to the other and you'll hear other winemakers praise his talent and devotion. You're not likely to hear Law himself praise either of these qualities, as he is a humble, self-effacing gentleman farmer at heart (in addition to grapevines, he also maintains an apple orchard on his rugged, unpretentious estate). Law basically led the charge in Virginia to focus on mountain-grown grapes—meaning he believed that fruit cultivated on hillsides produced better wines. He now has disciples all over Virginia.

3708 HARRELS CORNER RD.
LINDEN, VA 22642
540-364-1997
WWW.LINDENVINEYARDS.COM

Relaxing on the deck at Linden Vineyards.

VALHALLA VINEYARDS

At Valhalla, Jim and Debra Vascik offer a southwestern Virginia version of what Jim Law does at Linden farther north, but without the soft focus. This place is a winery first and a tourist destination second. Which doesn't mean you shouldn't schedule a visit, as the Vasciks have adopted Law's general winemaking philosophy and run with it. Some of the best wines in the state are produced at this rough-and-tumble facility, carved out of a hillside above Roanoke. Recently, a tasting room and event space, the Cellar Door, was added. It's a lovely stone structure perched on high ground, on a terrain already so hilly that Lance Armstrong used its roadways to train for the Tour de France. The views of the vineyards and the town below are commanding, but the wines are the real action here. Jim, a neurosurgeon, takes care of the estate's vines.

6500 MT. CHESTNUT RD.
ROANOKE, VA 24018
540-725-WINE
WWW.VALHALLAWINES.COM

Valhalla vines during their off season.

 The steep hillsides and spectacular views of Valhalla Vineyards.

Then he delivers the grapes to winemaker Debra. The winery was built according to a gravity-flow design—meaning that grape juice, once crushed, is never pumped into fermentation tanks; instead, it simply flows downhill. Gravity is all that's needed to move the process along. This ensures wines that have been minimally handled and are believed to be more flavorful (hey, they use this technique at Napa's Opus One, where the idea seems to have achieved some success). Debra then moves the wines into a cellar that has been blasted out of a hillside. It's a truly oldfangled approach, but you can't argue with the results, which are terrific. Debra manages to fill her reds in particular with robust red fruit flavors that are layered with spice, depth, and complexity. If you visit, don't miss the cellar tour. Many contemporary wineries simply throw up a temperature-controlled building and use that as a cellar. At Valhalla, they have a real *cave*: a damp, cool, dark place full of barrels that are full of peacefully aging wines.

Jim and Debra Vascik are still part-timers in the wine trade. But who knows how long that will last? They're achieving their greatest success with Rhône-style wines, which suggests that these wines—as many believe—stand the best chance of defining American regional winemaking's next wave.

 The winemaking facilities at Barboursville, which are the most extensive, sophisticated, and well staffed in the entire state.

BARBOURSVILLE VINEYARDS

While many of Virginia's other wineries are more or less mom-and-pop deals, Barboursville is not. Owned by an Italian conglomerate, it's much closer in spirit, not to mention layout, to a full-blown Napa Valley affair. Finding it is no problem; in fact, it's a real pleasure. You can meander (or zip, depending on how you like to drive) over narrow country roads. The University of Virginia is located nearby in Charlottesville, so you can enjoy all the advantages that an elite college town has to offer. Barboursville itself is fairly massive, by comparison with, say, Jim Law's almost quaint Linden Vineyards to the north. The winery is a full-scale facility, designed to crank out enough wines to support a national, er... drinkership (few other Virginia wineries have succeeded in getting their product such exposure). Winemaker Luca Paschina, Italian by birth, is Virginia's most professional winemaker. He also has by far the most

17655 WINERY RD.
BARBOURSVILLE, VA 22923
540-832-3824
WWW.BARBOURSVILLEWINE.COM

sophisticated facility in the state, as well as the most marketing muscle behind his product. This allows him more room to experiment than most. And experiment he has, shifting gradually away from popular American vinifera wine styles, such as Chardonnay and Cabernet Sauvignon, toward Rhône varietals, like Viognier, and Italian style grapes, including Sangiovese (always a tough grape to achieve success with outside Italy).

The tasting room is vast by Virginia standards, and the overall acreage is sizable. It features a unique tourist sight—the ruins of an eighteenth-century building designed by Thomas Jefferson; the winery allows the picturesque site to be used for performances and concerts. Hungry travelers will appreciate Barboursville's excellent restaurant, Palladio, which offers a level of dining that is at least five steps (and probably a few stars) ahead of the usual sandwich-café experience one gets at most regional wineries.

Because Paschina has been on the job for a while, he has the luxury of looking at the big picture in Virginia. To him, this means developing higher-quality vineyards. It's a typical old-world priority, but not one that every regional winemaker has the guts—or the time—to focus on. All in all, if you have to hit only one Virginia winery, this is the one.

BREAUX VINEYARDS

Virginia has a penchant for intense viticultural figures—men and women driven by an almost overwhelming passion for the vine—and Breaux is quite a bit more laid-back. Motor over here after visiting Linden and you might have your head slightly spun. However, just because this winery is operated by people who basically stumbled into the wine business, that doesn't mean the place is to be taken lightly. The wines are of reasonably high (if not scintillating) quality, the tasting room well-appointed and managed, and you can pick up a snack at Patio Madeleine, the winery's café. Unlike some other Virginia wineries, Breaux is located on basically flat land. It's easy to get to—you won't have to ascend a mountainside to investigate the wines.

OPPOSITE: The arches of Barboursville, inspired by the area's Jeffersonian architecture.

A Breaux vintage.

36888 BREAUX VINEYARDS LN.
PURCELLVILLE, VA 20132
800-492-9961
WWW.BREAUXVINEYARDS.COM

NORTH CAROLINA

BILTMORE ESTATE

This isn't quite next door to Virginia's winery hot spots, but it's such a spectacular location that it just had to be squeezed in here. Biltmore is a little bit of everything, all in one place. Yes, Biltmore is *that* Biltmore, the largest residence in America, home to the Vanderbilts. It's now a sort of vast historical site-cum-resort, complete with historic spots, an inn, restaurants, shopping, and plenty of other attractions. For our purposes, the winery is the focal point of this one hundred–acre property. Located in what was once the Biltmore Estates dairy, this classic structure, which actually boasts a clock tower, is where winemaker Bernard Delille oversees production of seventy-five thousand cases per year (that's a huge output, by American regional wine standards). Sample some of Biltmore's fifteen different labels in the tasting room, remembering that this is where they milked the cows back when the estate was run as an entirely self-sustaining enterprise. You are also free to take self-guided tours of the winery to observe the winemaking process in action. Spectacular gardens on the estate were created by Frederick Law Olmsted, the legendary landscape architect who designed New York's Central Park. Two sides of Olmsted are on display here: a rugged "shrub" garden that reveals his affection for the wildness of nature; and a formal Italian garden, which is all about the purity of Renaissance proportions. Of course, not everyone wants to cap a days of wine-tasting with a calming garden stroll. For them, Biltmore offers horseback riding, boating, and even a Land Rover Experience Driving School for off-roaders who want to hone their skills behind the wheel. Fans of the somewhat esoteric will appreciate that the Biltmore Estate was the site where the 1979 cult classic movie *Being There*, starring the late Peter Sellers and directed by Hollywood outcast Hal Ashby was filmed. But if movie trivia isn't important to you, no matter: the glorious Blue Ridge Mountains scenery should be more than cinematic enough.

1 APPROACH RD.

ASHEVILLE, NC 28803

800-543-2961

WWW.BILTMORE.COM

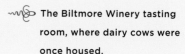 The Biltmore Winery tasting room, where dairy cows were once housed.

ℒABELS TO LOOK FOR

◎ LINDEN VINEYARDS HARDSCRABBLE RED

The Hardscrabble vineyards produce grapes that embody winemaker Jim Law's mountain-fruit ethic. This is a delicious, elegant, well-balanced red blend that might remind more than a few folks of a good Bordeaux Supérieur.

◎ LINDEN VINEYARDS HARDSCRABBLE CHARDONNAY

Chardonnay can be hit or miss, even in California. It is, however, America's most popular white wine, so most vintners feel a need to give it a go. At Linden, it's given a go and then some. This a very, very serious Chard, with legitimate Burgundian pretensions. No pineapple juice here; instead, the goal is a beautiful integration of pear and apple fruit with elegant French oak.

◎ VALHALLA VINEYARDS SYRAH

A rich, robust, peppery wine that typifies Valhalla's aggressive house style.

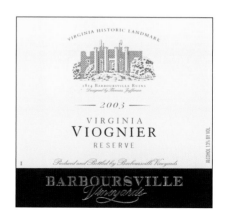

◎ VALHALLA VINEYARDS GOTTERDAMMERUNG

Owners Jim and Debra Vascik are big opera fans, hence the name of this Wagnerian red, a blend of Cabernet Franc and Merlot.

◎ BARBOURSVILLE VINEYARDS VIOGNIER RESERVE

Winemaker Luca Paschina has put a lot of faith in his hunch that Viognier, a white grape that has done well in France's Rhône Valley, will make better wine in Virginia than Chardonnay currently does. If

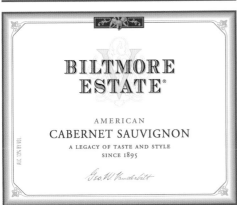

this fruity, textured version is any indication, then he might be right about the Old Dominion's *terroir.*

◎ BARBOURSVILLE BRUT

You wouldn't think that an Italian winemaker, Luca Paschina, would be able to craft a Champagne-style bubbly. Of course, Italians have plenty of experience with sparklers via their own version, Prosecco. This bottling, however, follows the Champagne formula—it's made from Chardonnay and Pinot Noir—but not the Champagne price: It costs less than $20. Light and refreshing, it's an ideal starter for a big meal.

◎ BARBOURSVILLE VINEYARDS CABERNET FRANC

It's easy to get into the regional-winemaking business and adopt Cabernet Sauvignon or Merlot as your signature red wine, until you figure out that your region isn't suited to either of those grapes. At Barboursville, although they produce many better-known red-wine styles, they're achieving what I consider to be a superior red grape for them, Cabernet Franc. This example has all the beautiful violet aromatics that the varietal is know for, but none of the harshly acidic green flavors that can hinder enjoyment of the wine.

◎ BILTMORE ESTATE CABERNET SAUVIGNON

For my money, this is the best red wine in North Carolina. And it's a Cabernet, which is surprising, as I've seen the varietal achieve limited success outside California. It's not complex, but it is fruit forward and relatively satisfying.

[AT A GLANCE: MICHIGAN]

CENTRAL ROADS: Michigan Rte. 22 is the main road
for many of the Leelanau Peninsula's wineries.

TOWNS TO VISIT: Traverse City, Leland, Suttons Bay

LOCAL FLAVORS:
The majority of cherries eaten in the U.S. come from Michigan,
and, of course, this fragile fruit is best tasted locally.

AVERAGE BOTTLE PRICE: $10–15

BEST TIME TO VISIT: May–October

WINERIES: 23

ACRES OF VINES: 2,000

YEARLY WINE PRODUCTION: 480,000 gallons

TOP WINES: sparkling wines, Riesling

WEBSITE: www.michiganwines.com

THE BOTTOM LINE:
Michigan still wines are still developing in terms of quality,
but the state is becoming a leader in sparkling wines.

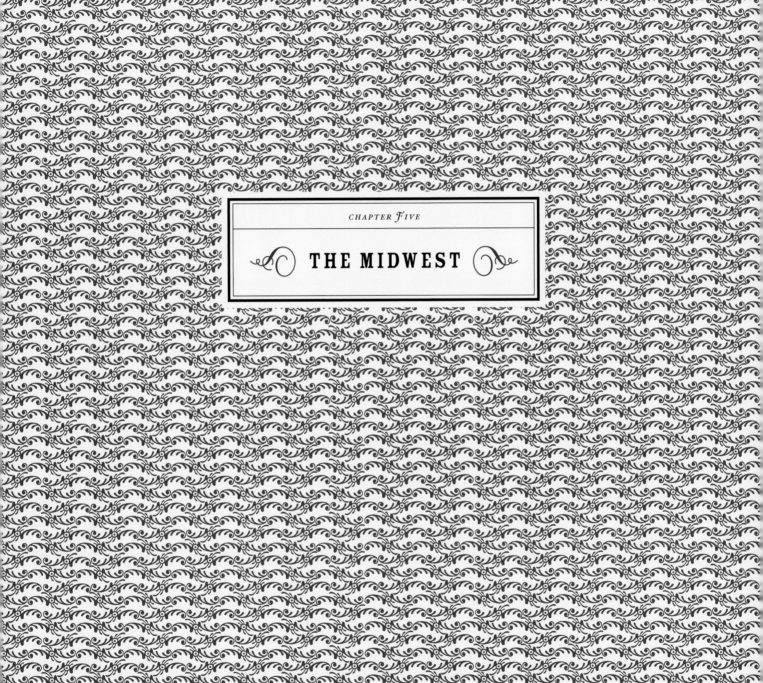

CHAPTER *Five*

THE MIDWEST

The view from Chateau Chantal, overlooking the Grand Traverse Bay.

TRUE NORTH

THE MIDWEST HAS FEW OBVIOUS THINGS going for it as a wine region. First, the climate tends to alternate between incredibly humid and hot in the summertime and brutally cold and snowbound in the winter. Spring and fall can be lovely, of course, but they just aren't long enough to create the kind of growing season that most vinifera grapes truly love: warm (but not muggy) between April and August, then more or less rain-free during a long autumn. Sure, it's possible to do the usual hodgepodge of native grapes and offbeat fruit wines. Chardonnay dreams, however, are elusive. The Midwest simply ain't the south of France. Nor is it northern California, with its eternal early autumn. Winemakers here face a steep challenge; this land just is not hospitable for traditional wine-grape growing.

But it's hard to dispute the beauty of the American Midwest, from the Ohio River Valley west, across the Mississippi and into the Great Plains. The area is often overlooked, especially in the wine world, where a certain coastal snobbery persists. If you've never visited this land of lush green landscapes, rolling hills, broad rivers, and vast meadows, you're missing out on a glorious slice of America. And, the cities of the Midwest are currently undergoing a renaissance as people are leaving places like New York and San Francisco due to the rising cost of living. Chicago acts as the centerpiece, but don't forget Cincinnati (Winston Churchill's favorite midwestern burg), Cleveland, Milwaukee, St. Louis, Kansas City, or Minneapolis/St. Paul. Even Detroit is making a minor comeback.

Speaking of Motown, one of the most scenic wine regions in the Midwest is Michigan's Leelanau Peninsula, a glorious finger of land that extends into Lake Michigan. About five hours north of Detroit, the Leelanau Peninsula

Michigan's main wine regions, in the northern reaches of the mitten-shaped state, are traditionally vacation areas for city dwellers. As such, there's not as much urban action as one might find in other U.S. wine regions. There is, however, plenty of stylish country fun to be had. The **LEELANAU PENINSULA WINE FESTIVAL** (231-271-9895) takes place each summer and provides a good opportunity to review the region's bottlings. The Traverse Epicurean Classic at the **GREAT LAKES CULINARY INSTITUTE** (9922 Fran St., Empire, 231-326-5134, above) is also a great place to sample the best of the region's wine and cuisine. Believe it or not, Michigan has a maritime history, as the **MARITIME MUSEUM** in the **SLEEPING BEAR DUNES NATIONAL LAKESHORE** reveals (231-326-5134).

is part of northern Michigan's traditional vacation country. This is where people who live in Chicago and in Michigan's large cities and towns have escaped to for decades, taking advantage of the gorgeous lakefront scenery, white-sand beaches, and the thoroughly relaxed vibe. You won't find anything that even vaguely resembles the traffic jams that are routine in Napa, but you will find a substantial number of dedicated vintners. They take advantage of the Great Lake Effect: The surrounding waters serve to mediate the colds in winter. The lakes also help to prevent damage due to early frost in spring and can give the vines an extra boost of warmth in the fall. This special microclimate gives the Leelanau a reprieve from the devestating arctic winds that blow down from Canada and deter most vinifera grapes in the region.

More than anywhere else in the U.S., the climate often strictly dictates which varieties are grown. With the exception of wines made from native grapes and French hybrid varietals, most of the Midwest doesn't do too well with reds. This is not as big a problem as it might at first seem. The truth is that a lot of Americans who drink wine prefer whites. So it isn't exactly the kiss of death to specialize—or to be forced to specialize—in whites. Furthermore, certain white wines actually require less cash and labor than reds. For example, if you want to produce Syrah, you will want to leave the grapes on the vines long enough to develop the deep, rich flavors that consumers now adore, then leave the grapes to age in oak for at least a few months. Leaving

Ripe Michigan grapes at harvest time (top) and the L. Mawby vineyards during the region's sometimes harsh snow season.

grapes on the vines in a climate like that of the Midwest's would be risky and would require a lot more management of the vineyards. Oak barrels, for aging, cost money. And by the time you're finished, even if you have managed to produce a decent Syrah, you'd have to charge quite a lot, by regional standards, to make a profit.

A SPARKLE ON THE HORIZON

Enter whites, particularly Riesling. Riesling vines tend to produce grapes in abundance (if permitted), and these grapes generally achieve good levels of ripeness early in the harvest season. Riesling is also not traditionally aged in oak. It can be produced in a wide range of styles, from quite sweet to rather dry. It's not necessary to charge a lot for a bottle to make your money back. Plus, it seems to do fairly well in the less-than-ideal viticultural climate of the Midwest. So do other German/Alsatian varietals such as Gewürztraminer and Pinot Gris. And, most important for the Midwest, white grapes can be made into sparkling wine. This could be the key to the region's future.

Why sparklers? Well, take a cue from the greatest sparkling-wine region in the world, Champagne. The world's best-known and most beloved alcoholic beverage is produced in France's most marginal growing area. If you were to make still wines from the Pinot Noir and Chardonnay grapes that go into Champagne, chances are you would end up with a wine not too dissimilar from what happens when vinifera wines are attempted in the

[BASE CAMP]

By plane, Detroit Metropolitan Airport is Michigan's hub, but it's pretty far from most of the state's wine trail. By car, the drive is about five hours, and M-22, a local route, circles the Leelanau Peninsula. Pellston Airport, near Mackinaw City, allows visitors to the Leelanau Peninsula to hop commuter flights from Detroit and Chicago. Lodgings are not a problem, as the area is crammed with B&Bs. **BLACK STAR FARMS** in Suttons Bay on the Leelanau Peninsula offers a bed-and-breakfast as well a host of other attractions, including a working cream and cheese production facility, a small winery, and horse stables (10844 E. Revold Rd., 231-271-4970, above). **THE ANCHOR INN ON THE BAY** (11998 S. West Bay Shore Dr., 231-946-7442) is a fine family destination in Traverse City; the inn, a combination of hotel rooms and cottages, has nearby beach access. And the **HOMESTEAD RESORT** (Wood Ridge Rd., Glen Arbor, 231-334-5100) offers comfortable lodgings and family-friendly activities.

Midwest. Many of the wines would be thin and highly acidic, lacking any sense or ripeness. But make them into a sparkling wine, via the traditional *méthode champenoise*—in which sugar can be added to aid fermentation and intensify the flavors—and you really have something tremendous on your hands. With sparkling wine, you don't even need to start with grapes that have fully ripened.

Larry Mawby has undertaken this noble task and pointed the way for the great state of Michigan at his Leelanau winery, L. Mawby. Since 1984, the winery has been focused almost exclusively on sparkling wine, produced in the traditional *méthode champenoise*, going so far as to import bottles from Reims. The resulting sparklers have been a great success. Certainly, there are competitive sparkling-wine producers in America—especially in California, the Pacific Northwest, and on the East Coast. But Michigan sparklers are among the best. Mawby is definitely a star in the Michigan wine scene, and he actively consults at other wineries, helping others to improve their sparkling-wine production. His marketing savvy is enviable, and his clean, elegant packaging stands out.

SAVORING THE HEARTLAND

Now, you might think from all this oohing and aahing over Larry Mawby that I'm infatuated with one midwestern winemaker to the exclusion of everyone else in the region. Well, it was insightful of him to recognize that all this climate and terroir were really going to produce, in terms of a nationally impressive wine, sparklers! However, the

Midwest can still take pride in much of the wine that isn't produced by Mawby. Anyone who wants to enjoy a relaxing, scenic tour through some of the most lovely and largely undiscovered wine country in America should head for the Midwest. The region is best in spring and particularly in fall, when the weather is ideal and there's college-football excitement in the air. How about this for a tailgating strategy: set up behind the Escalade in South Bend or Ann Arbor (home to the University of Michigan and considered to be America's definitive college town) and pop a few corks on the local quaffs. That'll get you some deserved attention—and properly promote the midwestern region.

There's more than just pigskin in Michigan to complement the local wines. This the home of the giant Sleeping Bear Dunes, where you can run up mountains of sand if you need to work up an appetite. At the Great Lakes Culinary Institute, the professionally prepared world cuisine is available in a beautiful new waterfront facility. For dessert, the National Cherry Festival in Traverse City serves up delicious cherry dishes, not to mention music events and parades.

Michigan is clearly the winemaking leader of the Midwest, especially when it comes to growing grapes. Over three-quarters of midwestern grapevines are in Michigan, with Ohio coming in a close second. While most midwestern grapes will become grape juice or jam, not wine, there are plenty of wineries—and enthusiastic winemakers—in Ohio, Illinois, Indiana, Missouri, and the Dakotas. Some have been more successful than others, but for the most part wines here are not yet at the stage of competing with wines from the more established regions of the country. But that doesn't mean they're not worth tasting.

In Ohio, the Lake Erie region is worth checking out. The Ohio Wine Producers Association has organized a special wine trail between Cleveland and Toledo that combines, of all things, wine tasting and bird-watching. According to them, there are more than three hundred bird species living in this area—along with about a dozen wineries. The most distinguished wines here, as with so much of the regional scene, are made from the Riesling grape. There are wineries clustered around Columbus, and also scattered between Dayton and Cincinnati.

Illinois also supports a growing wine industry, with more than forty wineries. Most are in the southern part of the state, between the Mississippi and Ohio Rivers. Indiana claims several dozen. Missouri lists quite a few more, most strung along the Missouri River Valley between St. Louis and Kansas City, an area that early German settlers likened to the Rhineland. In the late 1800s, the state was a leader in the U.S., second only to California, in production. Missouri wines are surprisingly good. Some of the still wines, especially the whites, are real midwestern standouts. And of course both St. Louis and Kansas City are vibrant cities, giving the whole Missouri wine industry a couple of solid bases from which to develop tourism. The Gateway to the West could prove in the end to be the Midwest's regional wine leader—depending of course on how many other wineries turn on the sparkler path in Michigan.

A view from the Leorie Vineyard.

TASTING TRAIL

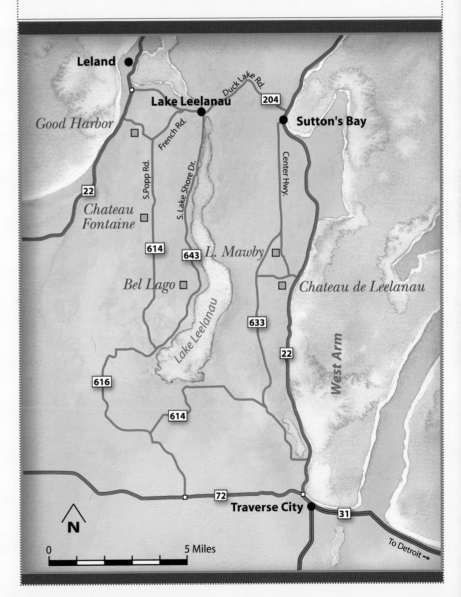

Leland

Duck Lake Rd.

Lake Leelanau

204

Good Harbor

French Rd.

Sutton's Bay

S.Popp Rd.

S. Lake Shore Dr.

Center Hwy.

22

Chateau
Fontaine

614

643

L. Mawby

Bel Lago

Chateau de Leelanau

633

Lake Leelanau

West Arm

22

616

614

72

Traverse City

31

To Detroit →

N

0   5 Miles

BEL LAGO WINERY

A good, standard-issue American regional winery, Bel Lago has been fighting the good fight in Michigan since 1987. The operation takes its name from one of two nearby lakes, obviously. There's the enormous Lake Michigan to the west and Lake Leelanau to the east. You're not going to find a whole lot of rich, heavy, California-style reds or whites if you drop by the pleasant tasting room. The winery's style leans toward lighter reds, such as Pinot Noir and Cabernet Franc, and a variety of whites, ranging from the offbeat Auxerrois to the ubiquitous muscat. Visitors to Bel Lago's tasting room will discover a simple, tasteful affair where contemporary art is displayed on the walls. During its history, the winery has won more than 100 awards.

6530 SOUTH LAKE SHORE DR.
CEDAR, MI 49643
231-228-4800
WWW.BELLAGO.COM

CHATEAU DE LEELANAU

Wine, for better or worse, sometimes seems as if it's largely a man's game (with certain glaring and admirable exceptions in extremely prestigious regions, such as Burgundy and Bordeaux). Not so here on the Leelanau Peninsula, where this winery is run by two women, Roberta Kurtz and Joanne Smart (they're the owners; there's a separate wine-making team). Chateau de Leelanau has gained some attention for its sparkling Riesling, called Andante. This is a solid indication that Michigan might have a real future as one of America's best sparkling-wine-producing regions. The recognition is even better for Chateau de Leelanau, which has been releasing vintages only since 1999. The winery isn't exactly the new kid on the block, however; Kurtz and Smart's vineyards have been under cultivation since the early 1990s. This is pretty typical—it usually requires about a decade for a vineyard to mature.

5048 SOUTH WEST BAY SHORE DR.
SUTTONS BAY, MI 49682
231-271-8888
WWW.CHATEAUDELEELANAU.COM

CHATEAU FONTAINE

An old-timer not just in Michigan but on the national winemaking scene. Owners Dan and Lucie Matthies have been in business since the 1970s, back when people weren't sure if California, much less Michigan, had a future in wine. It's a testament to the Matthies' gumption that their vineyards are now planted almost entirely with vinifera grapes: Pinot Gris, Chardonnay, Gewürztraminer, Pinot Noir, and Merlot. They were ahead of the curve in the '70s, and they remain today. In total, this winery has 17 acres planted to grapes. An advantage is the vineyards' natural southern exposure, which allows the grapes to soak up as much precious Michigan sun as possible during the growing season.

2290 SOUTH FRENCH RD.
LAKE LEELANAU, MI 49653
231-256-0000
WWW.CHATEAUFONTAINE.COM

Panoramic views from Chateau Fontaine, a former potato farm and cow pasture.

GOOD HARBOR VINEYARDS

The Simpsons are a family with deep roots in the Michigan agricultural tradition, but wine is a relatively new thing for them. Like many regional winemakers, owner Bruce Simpson did a stint in California, studying enology at the University of California at Davis before returning to Michigan to contribute to the state's winemaking growth. Of particular interest here are local favorites, such as a white blend labeled "Trillium," as well as a stand-alone Pinot Noir bottling. Simpson's philosophy is very contemporary: He believes that a wine's quality is determined in the vineyards, not during the winemaking process. Good Harbor is so devoted to this ideal that it has gotten involved with agricultural experiments in collaboration with Michigan State University. This might not sound like a big deal, but up-and-coming wine regions always prosper with university assistance. Interestingly, Good Harbor takes advantage of a natural process to get some vacation time. During fermentation, chilled crushed grapes produce crystals. At Good Harbor, they allow the winery to cool on its own by switching off the heat and heading someplace warm. When they return, the crystals are filtered off.

34 SOUTH MANITOU TRAIL
LAKE LEELANAU, MI 49653
231-256-7165
WWW.GOODHARBOR.COM

L. MAWBY VINEYARDS

Larry Mawby is a real visionary in the American regional winemaking world. So much so that it's probably not fair to label him "regional"; his sparkling wines are competitive with almost anybody else's (although they have a ways to go before they measure up to what they've been producing in Champagne for centuries). More regional vintners should have this intensity of focus. The winery is easy to check out during the year when it sponsors a series of picnics. Entranced visitors can sign up for the wine club, so that they never run out of these exquisite bubblies.

Mawby's current range of wines consists of ten sparklers and a pair of still wines (the sparklers make up ninety percent of his production). He gets creative with a whole list of proprietary names: Conservancy, Consort, Cremant, Fizz,

4519 SOUTH ELM VALLEY RD.
SUTTONS BAY, MI 49682
231-271-3522
WWW.LMAWBY.COM

The vines of L. Mawby Vineyards, where planned picnic events take advantage of the lush greenery and rolling hills.

Mille, and Talismøn. Larry Mawby is thoroughly unlike—pretty much the polar opposite of in fact—your standard-issue mom-and-pop regional winery proprietor. The man has panache—his Hawaiian-print shirts and straw hat defy Michigan's image as a chilly place.

LABELS TO LOOK FOR

◎ L. MAWBY BLANC DE BLANC

Possibly Michigan's best wine—and one of the nicest $16 sparklers you're likely to find anywhere in America. Stirring proof that trying to make good wine in a cold climate isn't a fool's errand.

◎ L. MAWBY BLANC DE NOIR

Blanc de Blanc means "white of whites," which indicates that mainly white grapes—Chardonnay, in most cases—went into it. Blanc de Noir means "white of blacks"—a white sparkling wine made from "black" or red grapes. Mostly Pinot Noir traditionally and in this case.

◎ L. MAWBY REDD

This is Mawby's answer to the legendary Cold Duck—or, by another, less infamous name, Rosé Champagne. Blended from Marechal Foch, an offbeat French hybrid grape, and Pinot Noir, this sparkler is designed to be enjoyed on the national Rosé Champagne holiday, Valentine's Day.

◎ M. LAWRENCE U.S. BRUT

M. Lawrence is Larry Mawby's alternative to *méthode champenoise* winemaking. He utilizes the cuvée-close technique (the secondary fermentation happens in a tank, rather than in the bottle), and the wine is made from grapes sourced from outside Michigan's Leelanau Peninsula. Having this extra label allows Mawby to evolve quality without being tied to the vicissitudes of an unpredictable, local grape supply. This wine is a classic blend of Pinot Noir and Chardonnay.

◎ M. LAWRENCE SEX BRUT ROSÉ

Another cuvée close wine, but one that comes out pink, thanks to the addition of Pinot Noir. Rosé sparklers are highly underrated and should be more widely enjoyed by people who are new to sparkling wine.

◎ BEL LAGO PINOT GRIGIO

Pinot Grigio is a popular northern Italian wine that sells well in America. In Michigan, the grape does better than Chardonnay, and although it tends not to be as plump or juicy as versions from the Veneto, it can showcase nice citrusy flavors.

◎ CHATEAU DE LEELANAU ANDANTE

This wine is further proof that Michigan does sparkling wine extremely well. This example is made from Riesling, and it demonstrates why, outside California, Washington, and New York, the state is a leader in American bubbly.

◎ CHATEAU FONTAINE PINOT GRIS

Pinot Gris is the Alsatian-French version of Italy's Pinot Grigio, and a grape that can perform well in a cooler climate. Chateau Fontaine's award-winning Pinot Gris is a textbook example of Leelanau white winemaking.

[AT A GLANCE: TEXAS]

CENTRAL ROADS: Highways 290 and 16

TOWNS TO VISIT: Austin, Fredericksburg, Stonewall

LOCAL FLAVORS:
Of course, Texas barbecue is world famous—especially the dry-rub beef style.
This is peach country, too, with roadside stands popping up all summer.

AVERAGE BOTTLE PRICE: $10–20

BEST TIME TO VISIT: May–November

WINERIES: 210

ACRES OF VINES: 3,200

YEARLY WINE PRODUCTION: More than 1.5 million gallons

TOP WINES: Cabernet Sauvignon, Tempranillo, Chardonnay, Viognier, Port

WEBSITE: www.texaswinetrails.com

THE BOTTOM LINE:
Texas has endured many false starts but now looks
poised to establish itself as the next big U.S. wine state.

CHAPTER *SIX*

THE SOUTHWEST

RUSTLE UP SOME WINE, PARDNER

MOST PEOPLE'S IMAGE OF TEXAS—and
for that matter, the entire Southwest—doesn't include
wine. But remember, the Lone Star State was once the
Republic of Texas, its own *country*. So it makes sense that
Texans would want their own wine country. These fiercely
independent folks just might feel a little sting at the
thought of having to truck in wine from their western
neighbor, California. They're much happier at making a go
of it for themselves.

There's been a coherent wine business in Texas for
roughly three decades now. Typically, Texans have
extremely outsized ambitions for their adventures with the
vine. In fact, ten years ago, just as the American wine boom
was taking hold, a lot of observers thought that Texas was
ideally positioned to be the next California—or at least the
next significant U.S. wine state. Americans were also

becoming more cautious about eating beef, and so ranchers
looked for alternative for their arid climate. There's winemaking in Arizona and New Mexico, but given Texas's size
and incredible financial wherewithal, not to mention its
relatively favorable climate, it seemed like a no-brainer. Get
ready for cowboy wine.

It didn't work out that way. Not because of curtailed
ambition, but because Texans rapidly discovered that wine
takes time. It isn't oil. It isn't cattle. It's one of those sophisticated products that takes time to get right. And for the
past decade or so, Texas has been struggling to get the formula down.

Which doesn't mean that you shouldn't get on a big ole
jet airliner and check out what Texas has to offer. My personal belief is that every American is duty bound to visit this
astounding state. As many a proud state native will tell you,

~~⟊⟊⟊ Wildflowers sprinkle the Texas countryside with color.

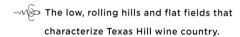
[LOCAL SCENE]

The Texas Hill Country is the center of Texas's burgeoning wine industry. It is also one of the most scenic and interesting parts of the Lone Star State to visit, located between two cosmopolitan cities, Austin and San Antonio. Check out **PEDERNALES FALLS STATE PARK** (2585 Park Rd. 6026, Johnson City, 830-868-7304) or **ENCHANTED ROCK STATE NATURAL AREA** (16710 Ranch Rd. 965, Fredericksburg, 325-247-3903) for great hiking and picnicking. Austin, with **THE UNIVERSITY OF TEXAS** and a vibrant local music scene, is a Lone Star cultural powerhouse. April visitors might want to check out the extremely urbane **TEXAS HILL COUNTRY WINE AND FOOD FESTIVAL** (512-542-WINE, above), sponsored by *Saveur* magazine. And if you find yourself in Fredericksburg (a terrific base camp town, well situated in the Hill Country), be sure to drop by the **NATIONAL MUSEUM OF THE PACIFIC WAR**, formerly the Nimitz Museum, named for the World War II naval commander (430 East Main St., 830-997-8220). Golfers will want to plan a tee time at the **WESTIN LA CANTERA RESORT** near San Antonio, home to the Texas Open PGA tournament (16641 La Cantera Parkway, 210-558-6500).

Texas holds a place of honor in the history of winemaking worldwide. Back in the late 1800s, when winemakers across Europe were in a frenzy due to a plague of phylloxera, Mr. T.V. Munson of Dennison, Texas, swooped in to save the day. A smart viticulturist, he sent good ole American rootstock, which is hardier and more disease-resistant, to the French so they could graft onto their vines. We might not have all the wonderful classic European varietals today if it hadn't been for this Texan's quick thinking. Today the state boasts numerous wine trails, scattered throughout the state. (Not only that, there are some *serious* straightaways on the Texas road system; meaning that, if you occasionally feel the need for speed in a rented Ford Mustang, you can . . . Well, let's just say you want to be careful—no point in leaving the state with a $100 speeding ticket.)

Fortunately for oenophiles who don't own personal aircraft, many of Texas's wine trails are concentrated in the region between Austin and San Antonio in East Texas, a part of the state that might surprise people whose impressions of Texas were formed by John Wayne movies, or the famous scene from *Giant* in which James Dean strikes oil. This part of the state is known as the Hill Country. It's relatively green with—you guessed it—lots of rolling hills, some jagged, low-slung mountain ranges, meandering creeks, and lots of pecan, oak, and cyprus trees. The high altitude is the saving grace from the rest of the state's sweltering heat; most important for the vines, the elevation keeps the soils cool at night. The Colorado River and the

lakes it contributes to also help. It reminds many well-traveled Texan winemakers of Spain. And not just on account of the landscape.

One of the Hill Country's most talented—and outspoken—vintners, Jim Johnson of Alamosa Wine Cellars, insists that the future of Texas wine is to be found in what he describes as hot-climate grape varieties. In the late 1980s and 90s, the quest was definitely on to produce California-caliber Chards and Cabs. But these old standards proved to be a California-wannabe trap. Texas's at times brutal climate won't support such a foolish undertaking. Instead, Johnson lobbies for Rhône grapes such as Viognier, and Syrah, and for Spanish varieties like Tempranillo and Grenache. This spirit of proud experimentation is widespread among the Hill Country's current generation of small-scale wineries. More established, older wineries also have begun to change their tune. Another new focus is placed on improving the overall quality of the grape supply. With this has come slightly downgraded expectations. Much of Texas now seems as if it would be content to become the American Languedoc, producing respectable bulk wines that can undercut volume brands from California. You won't find this urge in the Hill Country, where premium winemaking is the rule, nor will you encounter it in West Texas, where the High Plains region has actually been pursuing a premium model for many years. But you *will* find it in the space in between, where hills begin to give way to plains, and where there really aren't any tasting trails. Llano Estacado, for instance, has created what looks an awful lot like an Australian-style techno-winery, intended to crank out gallons of good, if not premium, juice.

Other longtime Texas winemakers such as Ed Auler of Fall Creek Vineyards have also climbed on the better-grape-supply bandwagon, bringing a somewhat more premium philosophy into play. Auler has seen Texas move through several boom-and-bust wine cycles. From his point of view, the state simply can't follow the currently popular Oregon model and aim to sell only small quantities of superpremium wine. Texas needs to enhance the *overall* grape supply, so that there's simply more decent fruit available to everybody.

Well, it's Texas. There are going to be differences of opinion. What matters to visitors, however, is the abundance of friendly wineries. There are several points of entry for wine lovers who want to trace Texas wine trails. You can start in Houston, rent a car, and drive west, hitting wineries along the way until you get to the Hill Country, where the trails proliferate. Or you can go to Austin or San Antonio and cut directly to the Hill Country chase. The truly intrepid will go to Lubbock and visit the High Plains first, then grab a commuter flight to the Hill Country. And, of course, you could always just take, oh, I don't know... a month off and drive across the state from east to west, visiting everybody before crossing the New Mexico border and getting started on *that* state's wineries.

A few tips: Geographically, Texas—and the entire Southwest—is gargantuan. If you're accustomed to relatively more compact regions like Napa and Sonoma, the Lone Star State can be daunting. Even in the Hill Country, wineries and wine trails can be hours apart by car. But hey, Texas radio is terrific, so enjoy the drive. My advice is to stick to back roads as much as possible, using the highways to cover larger distances. The way the Texas highway system works, especially around a big city like Austin, you can miss an exit and drive twenty miles before you catch your mistake. Fortunately, you can obtain maps of all the state's wine trails at www.texaswinetrails.com, which monitors the progress of the state's industry and compiles all the information on Texas wine that anyone could ever use.

LONE STAR NEIGHBORS

Texas is the anchor of the entire southwestern wine industry. But there are other states that produce the juice. New Mexico is where you might want to turn your attention next. What it lacks in national ambition it makes up for in breathtaking scenery and tremendous culture. In the grand scheme of things, the wines are still on a learning curve, but there's no reason not to sample them. Besides, with all the options that New Mexico offers for outdoorsy types—camping, rock climbing, kayaking, hiking, mountain biking—you can easily work up a thirst.

There are close to thirty wineries operating in New Mexico. The best known is probably Gruet, in Albuquer-

In the town of Fredericksburg, Robert and Patti Vander Lyn operate **ROSE HILL MANOR** (2614 Upper Albert Rd., 1-877-ROSEHIL, above), an elegant bed-and-breakfast modeled after a Charleston mansion (which just happens, in this case, to sit in the middle of a field, not on the coast of the Atlantic Ocean). You can relax here in the main inn by leafing through any of the thousands of books amassed by the proprietors. This is the place to stay if you're doing some Hill Country wine touring, since Texas wines are a specialty at the bar. **THE RODDY TREE RANCH BED & BREAKFAST** in Hunt (Highway 39, 830-367-2871) is located close to Fredericksburg, on the Guadalupe River. For visitors who enjoy a rustic, Old West vibe, **HAT CREEK CABINS** (Highway 29, 866-396-3399) might be a good fit, with actual cabins that have names like "The Wrangler" and "The Cattleman." It's located in the rather small ranching town of Menard.

[THE NATIVES VS. THE INVADERS]

WHY VINIFERA WINS

Fifty years ago, the world's best wine grapes —*vitis vinifera*— were not widely cultivated in America. If you traveled around the wine country in the Eisenhower Administration (okay, there wasn't much wine country per se back then, but there were vines), you'd have been more likely to encounter native grape varieties, such as Concord, which many people know because it's a widely loved juice wine. Or else French hybrids, such as Baco Noir. Times have changed since then, as the revolution in winemaking quality has swept across the land. Now, most winemakers interested in producing high-caliber wines have made the switch to vinifera varieties: Chardonnay, Cabernet Sauvignon, Merlot, and so on. For example, Joe and Vickie Greff at Blue Mountain Vineyards in Pennsylvania began with natives and hybrids, but changed over to hybrids and haven't looked back. This trend is everywhere. The results as are tough to argue with, as the world's best wines have been made from vinifera grapes for centuries. However, native varieties have one important thing going for them: their vines are resistant to phylloxera, the root louse that infamously devastated the vinifera vineyards of Europe in the nineteenth century. American native rootstock saved Europe back then. Today many vines around the world are grafted onto American native rootstocks in order to ensure against disease. So even though the wines made from native varietals are sometimes labeled as "foxy," due to their backwoods, rustic aromas and flavors, Americans take take solace in the fact that there might not have been any great vintages in Europe in the twentieth century and beyond without their humble, louse-resistant vines.

que (convenient to the airport), whose specialty is sparkling wine (the Gruet family is originally from the Champagne region of France). But because sparkling wines are often made from Chardonnay and Pinot Noir, still versions of these wines are also available.

Other notable New Mexico wineries include Anderson Valley Vineyards (the annual Balloon Festival is the occasion for the release of the special rosé), Black Mesa Winery, La Chiripada Winery, and Luna Rossa. The trick with New Mexico wines is to focus on wineries that produce wines only from vinifera grapes (as opposed to fruit wines) and that preferably source their grapes from their own estates, rather than buying them from California. You can obtain lots of useful information regarding New Mexico wines from the New Mexico Wine Growers Association Web site (http://www.nmwine.net).

Moving right along, Arizona is no winemaking slouch. What you will notice as you review the Southwest's regional wine scene is that vintners will often reference their state's Spanish heritage, insisting that wine grapes have been cultivated in the region for centuries, since missionaries from Iberia made their way through the area. Take this with a grain of salt. Yes, the Southwest has a proud winemaking heritage. But in terms of real quality, it's still in its infancy. As in New Mexico, high temperatures pose a real challenge, as does the scarcity of water sources. Thus wine growing is best situated on high, cooler ground near rivers or lakes.

Arizona's wineries can also be found online, at the Arizona Wine Growers Association site (www.arizona wine.org). The industry here is nowhere near as large as in Texas or New Mexico, but it is respectable. Two of the better-known operations are Callaghan Vineyards and Dos Cabezas.

Other southwestern states boast wineries, too. Oklahoma, for example. Even Nevada, probably more famous by far for the wine cellars of pricey Las Vegas restaurants than any locally produced product. Of course, as I've suggested here, the best way to take in the Southwest is to pick one of the three main winemaking states—Texas, New Mexico, and Arizona—and target some wineries or a wine trail in each. If you have a few months to kill, maybe you could take in the whole region, but plan to bring your pilot's license.

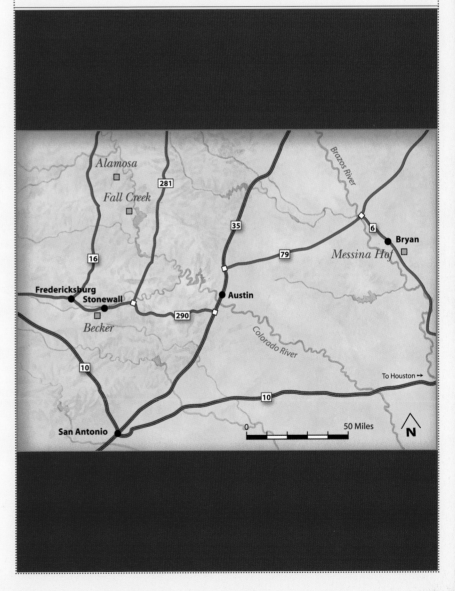

THE TEXAS HILL COUNTRY

TASTING TRAIL

 Texas wildflowers in the Hill Country.

~~⚘ A pest-deterring device
at Alamosa.

ALAMOSA WINE CELLARS

A little out of the way, as Hill Country wineries go but well worth the trip—especially now that the owners, Jim and Karen Johnson, have begun to improve the facility and offer tastings and tours. There's a certain cheerful intensity up here, in a part of the region called High Valley (twelve hundred feet above sea level). The focus in the vineyards is on hot-climate grape varieties: Viognier, Sangiovese, Grenache, Tempranillo, Mourvedre, and so on. You won't find any Chardonnay, but you will find Cabernet Sauvignon.

Jim Johnson had a circuitous route to his vineyard. After a first career in oil services, he decided to head off to California to learn how to make wine. It went well. Insanely well. Johnson wound up being mentored by Joe Heitz, one of Napa Valley's legends. He could easily have stayed in Napa and lived out a very happy career as a top-flight California winemaker. But Texas called, and Johnson responded. Now he has become the Joe Heitz of the Hill Country, a sometimes crusty but always cheerful opinionator, offering a steady stream of insights into what Texas needs to do in order to create world-class wines.

There are several ways to gain access to Johnson's wisdom. Check out one of Rose Hill Manor's Hill Country wine events (see page 109), where Johnson often speaks, or drive up to Alamosa and visit the oracle in his natural environment, surrounded by small vineyards that he harvests by (get this) golf cart and guards against marauding critters with a shotgun. The picture of confident Texas cool, Johnson is usually turned out in one of his winery's T-shirts or in a Hawaiian print. He represents the soul of this region, but he's no cowboy; this guy knows wine, and he is determined to wean Texas off its fantasies of Chardonnay and move the state toward Rhône and Spanish grape varieties—wines that he believes can flourish in the Hill Country's climate.

HIGHWAY 580

BEND, TX

325-628-3313

WWW.ALAMOSAWINECELLARS.COM

 Alamosa prides itself on keeping its vineyards healthy, with minimum impact and handling.

BECKER VINEYARDS

For my money, this winery is the highlight of the Hill Country, strictly from a tasting-room standpoint. Of course, the wines are also very serious (some have been served at the White House), and the production facility is among the best in the area. But its hard to get past the beautiful limestone barn, a reproduction in the style of the area's original settlers, that houses the tasting room. That same limestone that makes up the area's old barns comes from rich deposits in the Hill Country. This, along with a lot of granite, contribute to the area's terroir capabilities. This estate is made for wandering: There are quarter horses, orchards, gorgeous murals in the cellar (painted by local artists), and a beautiful field of lavender. Best of all, guests who plan ahead can stay at the property's original 1860s log cabin homestead, now offered as a bed-and-breakfast (for $125 a night).

Dr. Richard Becker, who still practices medicine in San Antonio, and his wife Bunny, run the show here, and they represent the new wave in Texas winemaking. They're well traveled, cosmopolitan, and savvy about marketing. They know that for the state to achieve its so-far fugitive promise, it needs to dramatically increase both the quality and national exposure of its wines. Becker also has an eye for talent; he and Jim Johnson worked together during the early days of Becker Vineyards, before Johnson decided to strike out on his own. *Wine Spectator* tagged Becker early on as a Hill Country player; his Estate Bottled Vintage Port was scored by the magazine as one of the best regional wines in America. Of course, the man has drunk enough wine from around the nation—not to mention fine Burgundy and Bordeaux—to know that there's plenty of work left to do, especially in the boom-and-bust world that is Texas winemaking.

HIGHWAY 290
STONEWALL, TX 78671
830-644-2681
WWW.BECKERVINEYARDS.COM

ABOVE: The Becker winery, housed in a nineteenth-century reproduction of a German stone barn.

OPPOSITE: Becker's Homestead Bed and Breakfast log cabin, built circa 1890, where a night's stay includes a bottle of wine and fresh baked goods.

FALL CREEK VINEYARDS

Fall Creek is so Texas that it's almost too much. The owner, Ed Auler, is the first in a long line of Texas ranchers who has roots in the state that go back generations to make wine. Cattle were his game before he and his wife Susan became enamored of wine on a trip to Burgundy. There is big game mounted on the walls of the tasting room, most of which his son shot, and which is an unusual choice of decor in comparison to the other wineries. But this is a beautiful, sophisticated, completely unpretentious place. Taking its name from a waterfall on the property that splashes into the bordering Lake Buchanan, Fall Creek has the feel of a grand French château, yet it is as laid-back as a villa in Tuscany. Beware: Texas weather can arrive very suddenly here. It's not uncommon to get caught in a thunderstorm you can spot when it's still on the opposite side of the lake.

Understandably, Ed Auler brings a quintessentially "bigger is better" view to what he considers to be Texas's wine-world destiny. It's hard to discount his ambitions, especially since he looks so determined in cowboy boots. The man is Lone Star aristocracy, and it shows in his desire to lead his state's wine industry forward. He doesn't think the boutique-winery model is going to work. Instead, he advocates a concerted effort to improve the Texas grape supply across the board, thus making high-quality fruit available to more winemakers with less risk involved. Will his plan work? Who knows, but he's a hard man to use the word *no* around.

1820 COUNTY RD. 222

TOW, TX 78672

325-379-5361

WWW.FCV.COM

 Wildflowers under the vast Texan sky at Fall Creek.

 Vines at Messina Hof, where the winemaking tradition can be traced back six generations.

MESSINA HOF WINERY & RESORT

Messina Hof isn't actually in the Hill Country. It's on the way to the Hill Country from Houston, not far from College Station, where Texas A & M University is located. This winery has been around for a while. It's a lively, almost circuslike place, presided over by the flamboyant Paul Bonarrigo and his slightly less flamboyant wife, Merrill. His family hailed from Messina, Italy, while her heritage is traced back to Germany. Hence the winery's multiculti name. The fun never stops at Messina Hof, where each year brings a dauntingly full slate of activities, from cooking classes to concerts to special harvest weekends. Visitors who have experienced Texas's long highway drives will appreciate Messina Hof's well-regarded restaurant, the Vintage House, as well as the Villa bed-and-breakfast, which offers comfortable lodging in ten themed rooms. A number of special packages are available, from romantic weekend getaways to honeymoon arrangements.

4545 OLD RELIANCE RD.
BRYAN, TX 77808
979-778-9463
WWW.MESSINAHOF.COM

*L*ABELS TO LOOK FOR

Ⓒ ALAMOSA WINE CELLARS EL GUAPO

An exciting red blend that defines Alamosa's style: blend hot-climate, red-grape varietals until you get a wine that knocks your socks off.

Ⓒ ALAMOSA WINE CELLARS VIOGNIER

A glimpse of the future for Texas whites—delicious, fruity, and distinctive.

Ⓒ FALL CREEK RESERVE CHARDONNAY

Probably the best Chardonnay in a state that probably has no business messing around with Chardonnay. This is the exception: big, rich, fruit flavors balanced by judicious use of oak.

Ⓒ FALL CREEK MERITUS

A superpremium, Bordeaux-style red blend whose first vintage was 1999. Fall Creek has high hopes that this boutique bottling will break Texas out of its regional rut and firmly establish the Hill Country as the state's preeminent wine region.

Ⓒ BECKER VINEYARDS VINTAGE PORT ESTATE BOTTLED

A powerful, fiery port that reminds me of a late-bottled vintage style from one of the great port houses of Portugal. This might be one of the areas to which Texas can look for future greatness.

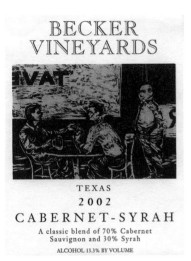

⌢ BECKER VINEYARDS CABERNET-SYRAH

A rich, meaty, Rhône-style red, full of dark red fruit flavors with a smoky, charry finish.

⌢ MESSINA HOF WHITE ZINFANDEL

Texas is hot country. It's also immune to snobbery. Which is why you should respect this tasty white Zin, in spite of what your wine-snob friends might tell you about white Zins (or, as they are sometimes called, "blush" wines). Frankly, there's always a place for a good white Zin, particularly when summertime and picnics and cookouts or barbecues roll around. Appropriately enough for a winery that has done a great job of marketing Texas wine to the rest of the country, Messina Hof's white Zinfandel has been declared among the best in the state.

⌢ LLANO ESTACADO SHIRAZ

Llano Estacado has placed itself at the forefront of Texas winemaking, pursuing both a premium and a bulk-wine philosophy. This Shiraz is an example of the bulk idea: It's produced from a large-scale, Australian-style "techo-winery" at the western edge of the Hill Country. A word to the wise: Don't let the "techno" tag turn you off— Aussie-style Shiraz is a natural in Texas's hot, dry climate.

CENTRAL ROADS: Interstate 70 runs east-west and acts as the main artery through Colorado wine country. It follows the path of the Colorado River.

TOWNS TO VISIT: Grand Junction, Gunnison, Whitewater

LOCAL FLAVORS:

Fly fishermen are well acquainted with Colorado's plentiful trout runs, which are happy casting waters for rainbows and browns. Colorado also produces some of the nation's most highly regarded lamb, as well as more exotic livestock such as bison.

AVERAGE BOTTLE PRICE: $10

BEST TIME TO VISIT:

Spring and fall deliver ideal weather; summer isn't too shabby, but daytime temperatures can rise into the nineties. Harvest is during September and October. Skiers will probably want to consider winter.

WINERIES: 48

ACRES OF VINES: About 500

YEARLY WINE PRODUCTION: 98,400 gallons

TOP WINES: Riesling, Chardonnay

WEBSITE: www.coloradowines.com

THE BOTTOM LINE:

Colorado benefits from an unusually good wine-growing climate. Not too long, not too short. Warms days, cool nights, and limited rain also help. The wine country here is at a higher elevation than anywhere else in the U.S.

CHAPTER Seven

THE
MOUNTAIN STATES

VINES IN THE SKY

THE REGIONAL WINE INDUSTRY in America's mountain states—Colorado, Utah, Idaho—is really still in its infancy. In Utah, for example, abstruse laws regarding the sale of alcoholic beverages has made it tough on the few wineries in that state. Colorado has fared better; it's the top dog in the region, home to almost fifty in a variety of areas. There's still a mom-and-pop flavor to winemaking in Colorado, but that's changing. Plenty of vintners have shifted over to vinifera grapes in an effort to match the national trend toward quality wines.

Regardless of what stage of its maturation as a grape-growing state this is still . . . well, they say God's country, which about does it for me. The whole Rocky Mountain range is pretty darn spectacular. Wine critics talk glowingly about "mountain fruit" in other wine regions, by which they could mean grapes grown on a small knoll to a craggy peak in the midst of an otherwise rolling plain of vineyards. (These sites are prized because the extra stress of growing on a hill leads to more complex flavors in the grape.) But when you speak of mountain fruit in Colorado, you're talking about serious mountains.

Most of the quality wine-producing vineyards are located on the western side of the Continental divide, and high altitude is the rule (football fans who have visited Mile High Stadium in Denver will know the feeling). How high? Try almost 5,000 feet in the Grande Valley, the largest growing region in the state. You won't find higher vineyards anywhere else on the continent and would be hard-pressed to find them elsewhere in the world. This altitude and harsh winters shorten the growing season, but they also limit exposure to problems, such as mildew and rot, that plague vintners in lower, more humid parts of the country.

Vineyards in the shadow of Lincoln Mountain, near Grand Junction.

Grand Junction maintains a comprehensive Web site that plays up the regional wine scene (www.visitgrand junction.com). The Grand Junction area boasts both the **COLORADO NATIONAL MONUMENT** (970-858-3617) and **THE GRAND MESA** (970-874-6600), which are a bounty for hikers and campers and outdoorsy types of every stripe. Golfers will want to check out the new facility at **REDLANDS MESA** (2325 West Ridges Boulevard, 970-263-9270). Any amateur paleontologists in the family? This is dinosaur country! In fact, there's a whole museum dedicated to the extensive number of prehistoric bones that have been discovered in the area: the **DINOSAUR JOURNEY MUSEUM**, in Fruita (550 Jurassic Ct., 970-858-7282, above).

Mountain state grapes are healthy grapes. This makes perfect sense, as a robust lifestyle is what draws people to Colorado in the first place.

ROCKY MOUNTAIN HIGH

All this adds up to some real geographical advantages. Colorado's vineyards are clustered on Grand Mesa, the world's largest flattop mountain, and amid river valleys. Characterizing the area's terroir are deposits of gravel and loam left by rivers — a mix similar to that of the esteemed Graves area of Bordeaux. These high vineyards benefit from the magic formula for good grapes: hot days and cool nights. In fact, during September and October — critical months for vinifera grape development in the Northern Hemisphere — daytime temperatures can drop up to 30 degrees once the sun goes down. Here's why this is a good thing: The grapes basically stop ripening, or "shut down," at night. This process helps to produce more complex and better balanced wines (too much hot makes for too much fruit, while too much cold yields wines that are tart and stingy with their fruit). The main drawback to this pleasant viticultural circumstance is that the Colorado wine country growing season is short, only about six months before the intense Rocky Mountain winter arrives. And, though snow cover helps insulate the vines, the winters can bring a killing frost once in a blue moon. Almost all of Grand Valley's vines were decimated by a severe cold spell in 1989, with night temperatures dropping to -22° F. In short, Colorado is blessed but cursed.

Colorado is also blessed in that its wine-growing areas are laced with rivers and streams. This, however, does not make up for the lack of a massive microclimatic influence, such as, oh, say. . . the Pacific Ocean. Still, these are fairly favorable conditions for grape cultivation, even with the late-season frost problem. Searching for a silver lining? The diseases, fungi, rots, and other nasty interlopers that plague incipient wine industries in America's burgeoning wine regions are mostly absent in the mountain states. For this reason, many vines were actually planted on their own vinifera roots. Planters didn't bother to graft onto American native variety roots.

Given these mixed growing conditions, the mountain states, as you might imagine, do whites better than reds. Great red wines require two things: relatively long growing seasons and winemaking expertise. In Colorado, for example, the growing season *can* be long enough, but only just, and winemaking expertise is only now beginning to come around. Is there hope? I'd say most definitely. The sheer number of wineries in on the game proves that. There's no question that the region is worth a visit, especially if you're a white-wine lover.

As for getting around, my suggestion is to make Denver, Boulder, or Grand Junction your base, and take I-70 west over to the Grande Valley region. Grand Junction, also served by its own airport, is conveniently situated right on the edge of the Grande Valley area, which is a few hours west of Denver and Boulder. Aspen is a good deal

〜 Harvesting in Colorado, a process involving both careful hands and efficient machines.

[FRESH FROM THE FARM]

ESTATE-GROWN GRAPES

When you see the phrase "estate-grown" on a label or in a winery's literature, it means that the fruit came from land the winemaker owns and cultivates—land that comprises the winemaker's "estate." Generally speaking, this is a stamp of quality, as it means that the winemaker—or someone who works for the winery, usually a vineyard manager—had full control over the growing conditions. What's the alternative? Winemakers can "source" their fruit from vineyards that they don't own from nearby or far away. This is often an economic decision; grapes grown offsite can be cheaper—because perhaps they come from a larger vineyard or are part of a surplus crop. However, just because a wine is not called estate-grown doesn't mean it's cheap plonk. The winemaker may well have chosen to go outside the estate because the other supplier's grapes provided that extra something the wine needed for the right balance. In that case, the grapes can actually cost more than they would if they were estate-grown. In any case, as long as the grapes came from the same AVA, the wine can be labeled accordingly. But if grapes are sourced from all over the state, the wine will be labeled, say, "California," rather than "Napa Valley." In the end, estate-grown grapes aren't always better, but they often are.

closer. The wineries here are fairly well compacted, so you can take in quite a few over a day or two.

As is the case when visiting wineries in the Southwest, getting from winery to winery in Colorado and the other mountain states can be a challenge. At the very least, it can involve some serious driving. Distances are just greater out here, and wineries are farther apart. The advice that goes in Sonoma doesn't fly; you need to do something other than simply find a stretch with twenty-five wineries on it and start tasting. Plan longer stays, basing yourself out of the nearest large city or town, and execute day trips to the wine country. This way, you won't feel compelled to drive hundreds of exhausting miles in a single day, and you can elect to break up your tasting and touring with, say, a Colorado Rockies baseball game, or some kayaking on the Colorado River.

The sweeping view from the vineyards of Colorado Cellars.

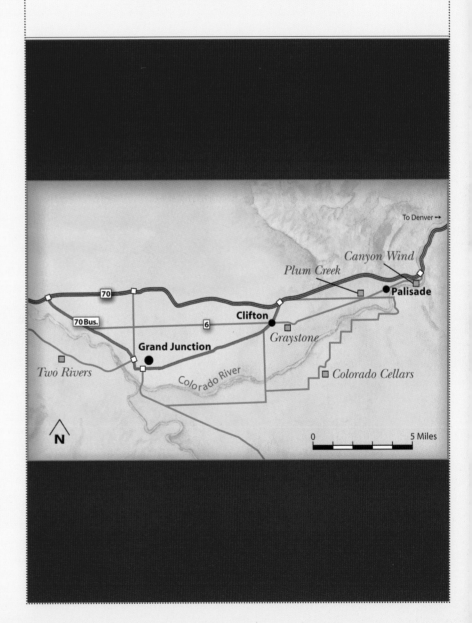

A picture-perfect sunset in the Grande Valley.

TWO RIVERS WINERY

This sprawling winery and conference center (plus a bed-and-breakfast) has grown up literally overnight—it's only been around since 1999. That makes it a pretty good all-in-one deal for Grand Junction wine-country tourism. Winemaker Glenn Foster deals only in premium vinifera wines, and the winery claims that it wants to ramp up production to eight thousand cases in the near future. That's fairly ambitious for a place that has only been in existence for five years. So far, Foster's reds, especially his Cabernet Sauvignon, seem to be garnering most of the attention.

2087 BROADWAY

GRAND JUNCTION, CO 81503

970-255-1471

WWW.TWORIVERSWINERY.COM

GRAYSTONE WINERY

Graystone, which opened in 2001, is an absolute Colorado newbie. So far, the focus has been on whites and, of all things, port (which can actually be an easier wine to produce than traditional reds because it is fortified with alcohol). Of course, at Graystone, they don't make port to improve on bad red wine. They make port because they love to make port. Now, this isn't vintage stuff that you'll want to cellar for decades. But it is a wonderful American alternative to drinking Portuguese products such as Late Bottle Vintage Ports early. If you visit, ask about the fortification process. If your timing is right, you might get a demonstration.

3334 F RD.

CLIFTON, CO 81520

970-523-6611

WWW.GRAYSTONEWINE.COM

Young vines (left) and an equine sculpture at Graystone.

PLUM CREEK CELLARS

Chardonnay Chicken, an iron sculpture, points the way into this venerable winery—well, venerable by Colorado standards. The vines have been under cultivation here since 1984. The scene at the winery is very relaxed. You're free most of the year to check out Plum Creek's portfolio of wines, everything from Cabernet Franc to a Sangiovese dessert wine. The winery currently maintains fifty-five acres of vineyards, not to mention what has to be something of a record for award-winning Colorado wines. It claims that it has been presented with 325 medals. Sometimes, pioneering American regional wineries can be tourist traps, but not Plum Creek. Quality leads the way here.

3708 G RD.

PALISADE, CO 81526

970-464-7586

 Plum Creek Cellars, which boasts a picnic patio and an antique-filled tasting room.

CANYON WIND CELLARS

A winery at forty-seven hundred feet above sea level? That's Canyon Wind. (Just for comparison's sake, wineries in Napa tend to languish around 1,000 to 1,400 feet above sea-level.) The vineyards here, located above the Colorado River, were laid out in 1991, but Canyon Wind's first wines didn't come along until the mid-'90s. That's remarkable progress for a regional winery, evidence of Canyon Wind's commitment. This is a technologically advanced facility, with an inviting tasting room that's open almost year-round.

3907 NORTH RIVER RD.
PALISADE, CO 81526
970-464-0888
WWW.CANYONWINDCELLARS.COM

Vines heavy with fruit at Canyon Wind (above left), and a rainy day at the vineyard, where weather hurdles inspire patience and ingenuity in the winemakers.

COLORADO CELLARS WINERY

An old-timer by Colorado standards, this winery has been in existence since 1978, producing a mix of fruit wines and vinifera-derived bottlings. The facility is large (Colorado Cellars claims it is the largest in the state), featuring spaces for banquets and wedding receptions, as well as tastings. The winery is tucked into a hillside, with enchanting views of fruit orchards and the town of Grand Junction. There are lovely spots to picnic on the grounds, including a gazebo. Family-owned, Colorado Cellars also produces what might be America's most entertainingly named wine, "Roadkill Red." No word if it's ever actually killed anybody (or anything). But the more time you spend on the wine trail, the more you learn to appreicate a winemaker's sense of humor.

3553 E RD.

PALISADE, CO 81526

800-848-2812

The Colorado Cellars winery, while large, is unobtrusive in the dynamic landscape.

LABELS TO LOOK FOR

CANYON WIND DESERT ROSÉ

Rosés are summertime wines, derived from the light-and-easy tradition of France's Mediterranean coast. Colorado isn't Nice, but this rosé is a good use of the state's not always reliable red-grape varieties.

CANYON WIND CELLARS MERLOT

Colorado is still finding its legs with reds, but that doesn't mean you should completely shy away from those wines. This Merlot, a repeat winner at the Los Angeles County Fair, is a tasty introduction to a wildly popular international varietal.

TWO RIVERS WINERY CHARDONNAY

Two Rivers has grand ambitions for the Grande Valley. That means a marketable white wine, and that means Chardonnay. This is a decent example of Colorado's ability to produce America's favorite white wine.

TWO RIVERS WINERY RIESLING

None of Two Rivers' wines are priced above $15. This basic Riesling, a solid bargain, is the winery's only gold-medal winner at an out-of-state competition (in Monterey, where they take wine pretty seriously).

PLUM CREEK CELLARS CABERNET FRANC

Plum Creek has been making wine in Colorado since the mid-1980s. It's safe to say that it has figured out this Rocky Mountain terroir.

Often, Cabernet Franc can be a great regional-American red to look for, as it can be enjoyed in a lighter style than Merlot or Cabernet Sauvignon.

℗ PLUM CREEK CELLARS RESERVE CABERNET SAUVIGNON
Sometimes, "reserve" just means "more expensive." Not in this case. Plum Creek's ambitious treatment of this great grape is emblematic of the winery's commitment to producing fine red wines "exclusively from fruit grown in Colorado." This does represent a real accomplishment because it's all too tempting for regional wineries to truck in out-of-state juice, especially when tricky, late-ripening reds like Cabernet are involved.

℗ COLORADO CELLARS CHARDONNAY
Chardonnay is, contrary to popular belief, a tough grape. At Colorado Cellars—the state's oldest winery—it's handled expertly, delivering a solid introduction to what the Rocky Mountain region can do with the world's best-known white.

℗ GRAYSTONE VINEYARDS PORT
Port, the famous Portuguese fortified wine, can be a real performer at American regional wineries. Why? Because it's not as completely dependent on grape quality as still wines.

[AT A GLANCE: OREGON]

CENTRAL ROADS:
Interstate 5 is the main artery flowing south from Portland, along the path of the
Willamette River. Many of the wineries can be reached via Highway 99.

TOWNS TO VISIT:
Eugene, home of the University of Oregon; Albany, where art galleries and
theaters are a good place to escape the occasional rain shower; McMinnville, a historic
town where you can see Howard Hughes's wooden plane *The Spruce Goose*.

LOCAL FLAVORS:
As with many wine-growing regions, wonderful fruit is abundant in Oregon.
Look for apples, apricots, and peaches.

AVERAGE BOTTLE PRICE: $10–50

BEST TIME TO VISIT: Spring or summer

WINERIES: 217

ACRES OF VINES: 9,000

YEARLY WINE PRODUCTION:
More than 2,400,000 gallons

TOP WINES: Pinot Noir, Pinot Gris

WEBSITE: www.oregonwine.org

THE BOTTOM LINE:
Oregon produces the world's best non-Burgundian Pinot Noir.
This is America's only all-premium wine region.

CHAPTER EIGHT

OREGON

CALIFORNIA'S CLOSEST RIVAL

THE PACIFIC NORTHWEST is the greatest success story in the modern history of wine. Okay, maybe that's an exaggeration. Australia is, on balance, perhaps a bigger deal. But, the Pacific Northwest has shown perhaps the most dramatic upstart in our time.

First off, it was never clear that the climate this far north, with its abundantly documented rainfall each year, would be able to sustain premium wine-grape cultivation. Nor was it clear that what is effectively a cool climate could generate the kind of rich, heavy wines that, these days, the international palate seems to go for and that naturally come from warmer soils. Add to that the immense capital expense required to get a wine industry going from what was effectively a standing start in the 1960s—when Eyrie Vineyard's David Lett took a chance by planting grapes—and you get an idea of the challenges that the region has met.

The second big reason to applaud what they've done up in America's rain belt involves an appreciation of strategy. There are a couple of ways to build a wine industry: on quality or on volume. The latter usually entails producing gallons and gallons of what's essentially unremarkable plonk while amassing expertise, then gradually beginning to enhance the product once the base is established. This is how California did it. Heck, this is basically how France and Italy did it, too, although they spent centuries evolving their wines.

Unfortunately, the bulk-wine scene has become very globally competitive. You really need a favorable climate—as in California, Australia, Spain, or southern France—to make a go of it. Otherwise, you'll be undercut right out of existence price-wise. On the American regional scene, Texas is experiencing this very problem right now, as the state tries to simultaneously develop a bulk and premium wine business.

Domaine Drouhin, situated in the Red Hills of Oregon.

The Pacific Northwest solved this problem by ignoring the subpremium market altogether. Almost all the wines produced in Oregon, as well as neighboring Washington, are considered premium wines; that is, there's very little product priced below the $7 to $10 range. Winemakers didn't have much choice: Oregon's climate in particular can be so unpredictable that there was no way the state was going to be able to crank out a lot of reliable wine year after year. Especially in Oregon, they gambled by aiming high from the get-go. And they surprised a lot of observers by pulling it off.

THE LITTLE WINES THAT COULD

In Oregon, winemakers decided—against all reasonable advice—that they possessed in a place like the Willamette Valley the ideal set of conditions for Pinot Noir. Yes, Pinot Noir, the great red grape of Burgundy, widely regarded by winemakers everywhere as the most difficult and fickle grape in existence. Even in Burgundy, Pinot Noir's spiritual home, the wines made from the grape are only really good two out of every five vintages. That's not a very good track record by modern standards. It's one thing in a place with a winemaking tradition that goes back to monks in the Dark Ages to try out the wine world's flakiest grape. It's quite another for an up-and-coming region to literally bet the farm on it.

But lo! it worked. Oregon doubled down on Pinot Noir and hit the jackpot. There are now plenty of French winemakers who express tremendous curiosity at what's

Stoller vineyard, the newest addition to Chehalem, where the vines are planted in red volcanic soil.

[BASE CAMP]

Spring visitors will want to consider staying at the **HOTEL OREGON** to check out the annual UFO festival, but also to enjoy a wonderful old hotel that's been around since 1905 (310 NE Evans St., McMinnville, 888-472-8427, above). The **BLACK WALNUT INN AND VINEYARD**, which opened in 2004, is a new thing in the wine country: a B&B that's more like a resort than what B&B regulars might be accustomed to (9600 NE Worden Hill Road, Dundee, 503-429-4114). There are only seven suites, so reserve early. A short drive from Portland, **SPRINGBROOK HAZELNUT FARM** (30295 N. Highway 99W, Newberg, 800-793-8528) consists of plenty of grounds to wander, along with four buildings designed in the Craftsman style that has been popular in the Pacific Northwest since the early twentieth century.

happening in Oregon, up there in the mist and fog, amid the redwoods. In a lot of ways, hitting a home run with Pinot Noir could not be a more Oregonian achievement. The state has always defined itself against the vulgarity of California, practically erecting border checkpoints to keep the sun-kissed superficials to the south out of their soggy Elysium. Oregon wineries are not like California wineries: The general aesthetic here isn't architectural big-shot grandeur; it's fade-into-the-landscape mellow. Lots of woods. Not a lot of parking lots for roving mobs of tasting tourists. The state also enforces some of the strictest labeling regulations in the country. Bottles labeled with varietal names like Pinot Noir must contain at least ninety percent of that varietal. Furthermore, generic titles like Rhône and Chablis that more lenient California wineries can get away with are not allowed.

Producing world-class Pinot is also a bit of a finger in California's eye. They make wonderful Pinot in the Golden State—beautiful, rich, and above all else, consistent. But critics have always insisted that they are more New World than Old World. The New World tends to focus on the process of winemaking that happens after the grape reaches the press, whereas the Old World takes a more holistic approach, giving great consideration to what happens in the vineyard. New World wines lean toward bolder flavors with high alcohol content; Old World wines express the more delicate and elusive flavors of their terroir. For California, being called New World is something of a backhanded compliment—yes, you're pioneers of a new style, but you'll never be France.

Then along comes Oregon, with its more challenging climate, and poof! Pinots in a more delicate, but no less powerful, style. Oregon Pinots display flavors ranging from wet earth to, believe it or not, manure. They also can have the mineral notes so characteristic of terroir in France and are one of the few American wines that age well. The soil makeup of glacial till and rich topsoil may have something to do with the grape's success here, as well as the cooler temperatures and long, moderate growing season. It was Burgundy, sort of, just displaced some six thousand miles. So impressed, in fact, were the Burgundians themselves that some of them even developed winemaking partnerships with the Oregonians.

PACK YOUR BAGS FOR
THE PACIFIC NORTHWEST

The tasting trail to zero in on in Oregon is the Willamette Valley. The Willamette Valley is shaped by the course of the Willamette River, which runs from Portland to Eugene, between the Coast Range (separating the valley from the Pacific) and the Cascade Mountains (on the other side of which resides the hotter interior of the state). One of the things that the Willamette has going for it has nothing to do with the wine boom, but everything do with making it possible: floods that occurred tens of thousands of years ago, when the last Ice Age was ending. These floods basi-

cally pilfered volcanic soil from Washington—and volcanic soil, as anyone who has ever tasted a tomato from Italy can attest, can yield some phenomenal produce, especially when it comes to grapes. (This might be why the Willamette Valley is a source of such an interesting American terroir.) It also helps that the Coast Range and the Cascade Range bound the valley to the east and west, respectively. These mountains have a strong effect on the region's microclimate.

The best time to visit Oregon is in the spring, summer, and early autumn, pretty much a year-round destination, although during any given week, you'll have to contend with the possibility of rain. (It's worth noting, however, that the weather can get toasty during the daytime, so be sure to bring the sunscreen along.)

This is an extremely peaceful part of the country. It retains an unspoiled quality and hasn't yet been overrun by tourists. Oregonians want to keep it that way. In their major cities, they've legislated against urban sprawl, and in the vineyards, they have adopted a sustainable-agriculture model. Visitors tend to come away from touring Oregon feeling simultaneously soothed and exhilarated.

As is the case with much of the Pacific Northwest, Oregon can boast both mountains and beaches, with plenty of rolling hills and fertile valleys in between. And, speaking of agriculture, the wines are not the only premium product here—Oregonians take pride in their organic produce, which can be found at roadside stands

Quarter Mile Road vineyard, the original vineyard at Adelsheim and sheltered by the Chehalem mountains.

and farmer's markets across the state. The Tillamook Dairy, located about an hour west of Portland, has been crafting its signature cheeses for more than a century, and the mild weather on the coast gives the cranberries that grow there a unique bright color. Oregon has long been a mecca for outdoor enthusiasts. One of America's most spectacular natural places, the Columbia River Gorge, can be found not far from wine country. As the Columbia River nears the coast it opens up into this dramatic eighty-mile-long canyon whose walls can reach up to four thousand feet and provide rock climbers with a formidable challenge. A bit south, hikers and bikers should take a detour on the Wheaton ferry across the Willamette River to the Willamette Mission State Park. The area is also a hospitable destination for travelers who are less dependent on adrenaline highs. In the Willamette Valley you can see more covered bridges than in any other place west of the Mississippi River.

The driving here is marvelous—as long as you're not sloshing through a shower. Once you get clear of the cities, you can duck off the highways and explore winding country roads. Probably not the region in which to rent a convertible, however. But who knows? Maybe you'll get lucky.

Harvest time at Argyle, where grapes come from three separate vineyards.

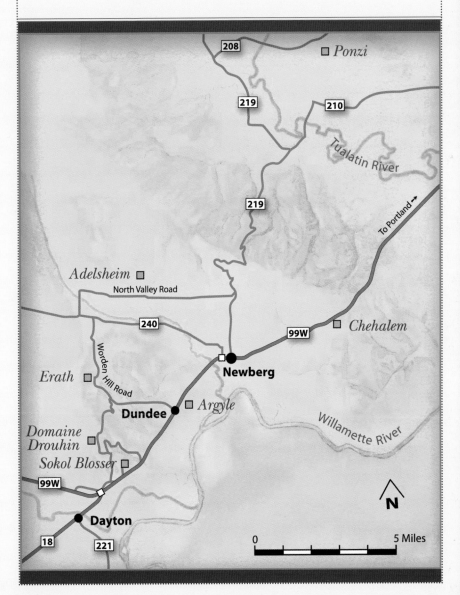

PORTLAND

Argyle grapes are chilled overnight before crushing, preserving the fruit characteristics and limiting oxidation.

THE WILLAMETTE VALLEY

TASTING TRAIL

208 · *Ponzi*

219 · 210

Tualatin River

To Portland →

Adelsheim ·
North Valley Road

240 · 99W · *Chehalem*

Erath ·
Worden Hill Road · **Newberg**

Argyle
Dundee ·

Domaine Drouhin
Sokol Blosser · *Willamette River*

99W

18 · 221 · **Dayton**

N

0   5 Miles

Argyle's Knudsen Vineyard, which is at a high elevation and provides grapes for the winery's sparkling wine.

ARGYLE WINERY

Winemaker Rollin Soles is a product of the American wine boom. A Texan, he obtained a microbiology degree from Texas A & M (a university that is now near the heart of that state's wine industry), then moved on to UC Davis, and later worked at several prestigious California wineries before starting his own with Brian Croser, an Australian who saw Oregon's potential. Established in 1987, Argyle now produces some of Oregon's most highly regarded Pinots in a variety of bottlings, from basic entry-level right on up through small-production, single-vineyard wines. In a single vineyard label, you can taste the purest expression of a certain terroir since grapes from such a defined geographic area only are used. Here that terroir comes through as delicious woodsy overtones. The winery itself is located in a restored Victorian mansion, in the town of Dundee, which considers itself the civic embodiment of the Oregon winemaking philosophy: great wines, no pretense.

691 HIGHWAY 99W
DUNDEE, OREGON 97115
503-538-8520
WWW.ARGYLEWINERY.COM

PONZI VINEYARDS

Dick and Nancy Ponzi, the cofounders of this three-decade-old winery, are a pair of plucky Oregon pioneers. A second generation has now joined them in the venture. Ponzi is ambitious, striving to fully express the Oregon wine-country lifestyle through the winery, its restaurant, and wine bar (these last two, taken together, comprise the Ponzi Culinary Center). The winery and tasting room are typically down-to-earth Oregon affairs. Don't look for any fancy flair decor here. The wines are also unpretentious, but they are anything but ordinary. Ponzi is a must-visit because this is one of a handful of wineries that gave birth to the current Oregon wine industry. Not incidentally, Beaverton is also home to athletic shoe pioneer Nike.

14665 SW WINERY LN.
BEAVERTON, OREGON 97007
503-628-1227
WWW.PONZIWINES.COM

ABOVE: The Ponzi winery, where sustainable growing practices preserve the local environment (left), and harvest at Ponzi.

Chehalem's Stoller vineyard, which boasts a spectacular view of Mount Hood.

CHEHALEM

The principals behind this always wonderful producer are William and Cathy Stoller and co-owner and winemaker Harry Peterson-Nedry. Like Adelsheim, the game here is to schedule your visit in advance—completely worth the trouble, as you'll receive the kind of personal introduction to the vineyards and wines of this terrific estate in a way that's free of the usual tasting-room throngs that can cause bottlenecks in other regions. The winery maintains three vineyards, each yielding distinct fruit: Ridgecrest (the original); Stoller (the newest); and Coral Creek (the vineyard you will see if you visit the winery). There is no tasting room at the winery, but as is the case with much of Oregon, if you call ahead, you can set something up.

31190 NE VERITAS LN.
NEWBERG, OREGON 97132
503-538-4700
WWW.CHEHALEMWINES.COM

~w&c>~ *LEFT AND BELOW:* Erath vineyards, where owner Dick Erath maintains that the fruit and growing process is responsible for the quality in his wines.

ERATH VINEYARDS

This Oregon winery may seduce the cheapskate in you. Oregon wines are usually anything but cheap, but they're not generally terrifyingly expensive, either. Erath makes a basic Pinot Noir that sells for around $15. It's the best possible introduction one could have both to a winery that's been around since the early 1970s and to the Oregonian style of Pinot Noir in general. Dick Erath practically invented the Oregon wine business, and he continues to be one of the state's prime movers. He recognized early on that the state's apparent drawbacks as a premium winemaking region were actually hidden blessings. Tough conditions can often lead to superior wines, as the grapevines must struggle to survive. All along, Erath's ambition was to do in Oregon what had been done in Burgundy: produce superb wines in a marginal area that would wow the critics. He has succeeded, dramatically. After a rocky period in the 1980s, when it seemed as if the state might never live up to its alleged potential, Oregon and Erath, in particular, have been on a tear since the 1998 vintage. Erath has come a long way since 1967, when he was a figure in the winemaking wilderness, living in a log cabin and presiding over the production of a mere 216 cases. These days, he's up to 35,000. The tasting room here is the very picture of a laid-back, picnic-friendly scene. Views of the Dundee Hills and beyond to Mt. Hood and Mt. Jefferson make it the perfect place for a leisurely tasting

9409 NE WORDEN HILL RD.
DUNDEE, OREGON 97115
503-538-3318
WWW.ERATH.COM

SOKOL BLOSSER WINERY

"I see wine growing in Oregon as a risk/reward situation; the challenges are great, but so is the opportunity to create something really special. That is my goal at Sokol Blosser," says Russ Rosner, the winemaker at Sokol Blosser, a winery that has been around since 1977, in Dundee. His thoughts encapsulate the Oregon wine experience: challenging conditions often make for better wines. This has been proven true at Sokol Blosser for decades now (and especially in the string of wonderful vintages since 1998). And if you want to see a winery that's so mellow it practically recedes into the Red Hills of Dundee, this is your stop. Here, the policy is to make excellent wines while practicing sustainable growing practices, minimizing the impact on the land. This means that there are no synthetic fertilizers or chemicals used, and the owners are eager to point out the different kinds of wildlife, from bees to red-tailed hawks, that live among the vines.

5000 NE SOKOL BLOSSER LN.
DUNDEE, OREGON 97115
503-864-2282
WWW.SOKOLBLOSSER.COM

ABOVE: Sokol Blosser vineyards, where a number of environmentally friendly and sustainable growing practices have led to the winery's being certified as officially "green."

DOMAINE DROUHIN OREGON

Wine-country vets accustomed to swinging their cars into parking lot after parking lot, up and down a region's main drag, then tasting away, might wonder why so many of Oregon's premium wineries require advance work to secure an invitation. It's simple: That's the way they do premium winemaking in Europe (the tasting room is an American invention). Now, tasting rooms aren't a bad thing, but if most of what you produce is high-quality, relatively high-priced wine, you're not going to benefit from big tasting-room crowds since the crowds rarely spend that much per bottle. You need visitors who have come to you, eager to digest your philosophy and pay for your premium product. The Drouhins, a Burgundy wine family, bought into Oregon, literally and early, in 1987. In Burgundy, vintners typically operate as negociants, buying grapes and wine from growers and other producers, then marketing them under their own labels. Domaine Drouhin Oregon is a slightly different story, because the Drouhins have more of a direct ownership stake in their estate. Joseph Drouhin—he runs Maison Joseph Drouhin back in the old country—has his daughter, Véronique Drouhin-Boss, in charge of the winemaking here. Her touch is sure and competent, especially with the estate's fantastic Pinot Noirs. Her overall philosophy of limited intervention in the winemaking process dovetails perfectly with Oregon's ethos. Of course, the Drouhins are far from hippy-trippy, escape-from-California types. They are as French as can be. There is a very Burgundian feel to the vineyards that are planted here. At most wineries, you will find the physical facilities surrounded by vines. At Drouhin, site is considered more essential, so the vines are planted where the winemaker and the vineyard manager think they will do best. This leads to a patchwork quilt look that, to be honest, can't be appreciated as much on foot as from the air. And Oregon, ever adaptable, has welcomed the Drouhins' presence. If you visit the winery's Web site, you can get GPS coordinates to find the place. Now *that's* Oregon for you.

P.O. BOX 700

DUNDEE, OREGON 97115

503-864-2700

WWW.DOMAINEDROUHIN.COM

 Domaine Drouhin, where the vineyards are densely planted and require special French-made tractors for harvesting.

ADELSHEIM VINEYARD

Adelsheim is one of Oregon's most important wineries. Unfortunately, you can visit only if you call ahead. It's worth the effort. However, if that doesn't seem like your style, the winery hosts two open houses per year, one over Memorial Day weekend, the other during Thanksgiving. The facility is a studiously low-key affair, designed according to the gravity-flow model, which basically means that wines are manipulated through the winemaking process almost entirely by the simple force of gravity. The idea is such that minimal interference, or handling, leads to a far superior product. If Adelsheim's vintages are any indication, gravity flow is the way to go. The winery favors groups of less than twenty people and charges around $10 for a relatively comprehensive tasting.

16800 NE CALKINS LN.
NEWBERG, OREGON 97132
503-538-3652
WWW.ADELSHEIM.COM

ABOVE: Adelsheim's Bryan Creek Vineyard, which lies on the slope of Chehalem Mountain and produces fruit with intense, ripe flavors.

The Ribbon Springs Vineyard, which has sandstone-based soil and is an important provider of Pinot Gris grapes to Adelsheim.

LABELS TO LOOK FOR

ⓒ ERATH PINOT NOIR

A textbook, entry-level Oregon Pinot: soft but expressive, vibrant but not overpowering, fruity but not syrupy. A lot of balance and terroir for the price.

ⓒ DOMAINE DROUHIN OREGON PINOT NOIR

Drouhin's winemaker, Véronique Drouhin-Boss, has adapted the terroir Burgundy model to the New World. She pays more attention to what goes on in the vineyards, perhaps more than most other American winemakers. This is another fantastic introduction to what Oregon can do with one of Europe's classic grapes.

ⓒ ARGYLE PINOT NOIR

Argyle Pinots are some of Oregon's finest. At the higher end they can be pricey, but they're incredibly plush, aromatic, and rich. This is the basic model.

ⓒ ARGYLE "NUTHOUSE" PINOT NOIR

A wine that's totally over-the-top with its brash, exuberant blueberry and black-cherry fruit. This is the flamboyant side of Oregon Pinot Noir, from a producer whose lineup of single-vineyard bottlings rarely fails to impress.

ⓒ PONZI PINOT NOIR RESERVE

Step up to a reserve wine. This Pinot is what Oregon is all about—a beautiful, juicy bottling, with layers of complexity. Like a great red Burgundy, this possesses tastes of cherry and chocolate.

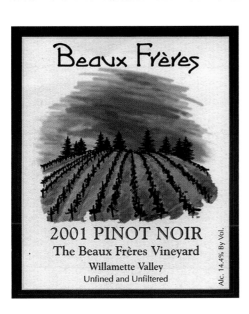

ADELSHEIM OREGON PINOT NOIR

The coiffed, bare-shouldered lady on the label is Diane Lett, a member of the Adelsheim extended family. She's the inspiration for this easygoing Pinot, whose soft, smoky aromas and bright cherry flavors are punctuated by plenty of black pepper on the finish. Looking for something to go with the Pacific Northwest's renowned salmon? Barbecue the salmon and serve with this wine.

REX HILL PINOT NOIR

There's a compelling core of raspberry and cherry fruit here, along with soft vanilla notes (from the oak the wine was aged in). The peppery finish wants to meet up with a chicken, prepared Peruvian-style, with lots of spices. Or Cajun food.

BEAUX FRÈRES VINEYARD PINOT NOIR

Oregon at its absolute best here. In a few years, the gobs of black cherry and cardamom spice should have blended nicely with the brisk acidity and complex mineral undercurrent to produce a magnificent quaff.

SOKOL BLOSSER WILLAMETTE VALLEY PINOT NOIR

This is Sokol Blosser's basic Pinot. At around $25, it's a superb bargain. Unlike some Pinots, this is a blend; the grapes come from a variety of different vineyards, rather than from a single parcel. Typical Willamette flavors of cherries abound, with a nice kick from the oak barrels.

[AT A GLANCE: WASHINGTON]

CENTRAL ROADS:
Highway 12 is your friend when traveling through the Walla Walla region.

TOWNS TO VISIT:
Walla Walla is the biggest city in the area, or you can catch a rodeo in Yakima.
In the tri-cities of Richland, Pasco, and Kennewick, you can see celebrations
of the bicentennial of the Lewis and Clark expedition.

LOCAL FLAVORS: Sockeye salmon, Olympia oysters, Dungeness crab, and apples.

AVERAGE BOTTLE PRICE: $10–$20

BEST TIME TO VISIT: Year round

WINERIES: 240

ACRES OF VINES: 29,000

YEARLY WINE PRODUCTION: 17 million gallons

TOP WINES: Merlot, Cabernet Sauvignon, Riesling

WEBSITE: www.washingtonwines.com

THE BOTTOM LINE:
Second only to California, Washington has succeeded with the
all-premium model but spans a broader range of varieties than Oregon.

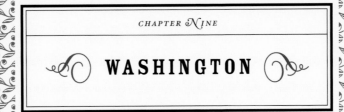

CHAPTER NINE

WASHINGTON

AMERICA'S UNEXPECTED BORDEAUX

LIKE NEIGHBORING OREGON, Washington also succeeded against the odds, with a style of wine that countered what everyone thought they were supposed to be drinking. Bold, high-alcohol Napa Cabs were believed to be the rule, at least as far as American winemaking went. Don't mess with Cab, Washington! But Washington did, and the results impressed a lot of folks. As Oregon Pinot Noir is to red Burgundy, Washington Cabernet is to red Bordeaux. Washington pioneered a lighter, more refined style of Cabernet than what California had traditionally produced—fruity and fresh but not overwhelming, and certainly not excessively dense or alcoholic.

Washington is fortunate in that the rains that typically beset the state each year seem to always hold off just long enough for its Bordeaux grapes to ripen (once you get away from the eternally moist and mild coast, that is). Combine that with a growing season that perfectly combines warm days and cool nights, a northerly latitude that exhibits more hours of sunshine, rough winters that don't get underway until November, and you have a formula for wines of grace, power, and beauty. The region is situated around the 47th Parallel, the same latitude as the Loire Valley and Alsace—a fact vintner here love to quote to their counterparts in Calirofnia. (Note also that, contrary to popular perception, all of Washington is not as soggy as Seattle; there are inland expanses that are effectively deserts. This is why you will find some of the country's most extensively irrigated vineyards here.) Volcanic ash from Mt. St. Helens contributes a unique factor to the terroir. Most important, don't forget, as in Oregon, the game here is not cheap plonk. Washington goes for the gold.

As with many U.S. states, Washington can date its winemaking heritage back to the late 1800s. This might lead you to believe that if a gold prospector or down-on-his-

~~ L'Ecole 41, which has a landscape unlike either California or East Coast wineries.

A visit to Washington wine country can easily begin in Seattle. The city's new public library is among the most touted buildings in the recent history of American architecture. Designed by Rem Koolhaas, this striking new structure is just the latest reason to visit one of the country's most vibrant metropolises. From the famous **PIKE PLACE MARKET** (1531 Western Avenue, 206-682-7453), where the locals buy their fresh fish, to the Seattle Symphony Orchestra at **BENAROYA HALL** (200 University St., 206-215-4747), Seattle is an easily managed feast of indoor and outdoor activities. In Walla Walla, fans of engineering will not want to pass up a visit to **GRAND COULEE DAM** (Highway 155, 509-633-9265). The **WHITMAN MISSION** (328 Whitman Mission Rd., 509-522-6357, above) commemorates the brave pioneers who established the Oregon Trail but confronted the region's native peoples in the process, leading to tensions that ultimately compelled the U.S. government to bring Oregon into the nation.

luck farmer planted a little grape patch a century ago, then that was the genesis of a multibillion-dollar industry. The truth is that serious wine-grape cultivation in Washington, as well as serious winemaking, didn't really get going until the 1960s, so the business is still relatively young here.

But that's a typical tale. Given the proximity of Prohibition, the Depression, and World War II, whatever indigenous American wine industry there was—in a country that didn't drink much wine and had no real homegrown wine culture—it's easy to understand why it took the better part of a century for American vintners to find themselves, so to speak. As the country became more affluent, and as the cultural revolution kicked off in the 1960s—and especially as Americans began to travel to dirt-cheap, wine-soaked Europe after the war—winemaking began to seem less like agricultural drudgery and more like an enviable way of life. The ethos was pioneered in California, but as that state became more and more commercial, it was only natural that some winemakers would seek to mark out new territory.

THE AGE OF DIONYSUS

During the Age of Aquarius decade, countless exiles from the establishment sought to capture a little Dionysian energy and turned to winemaking. These pioneers then formed the nucleus of Washington's present-day wine industry. Of course, it was slow going in the '60s and '70s, and even into the '80s. But by the '90s, premium wine-making had really taken off. Washington rode the decade expertly. Now, a new winery opens every few weeks, and the Washington wine industry believes that there is almost endless opportunity to grow. It's possible that in the near future vineyards could overtake orchards and displace the apple as Washington's most famous product.

A good starting point for Washington wine-country tourism is the Walla Walla region. Walla Walla (say it, it's fun) sits on the banks of the Columbia River, the border with Oregon to the south. Walla Walla is a ways inland from the coast, about three hours southeast of Seattle. The Yakima Valley, another region, sits between Walla Walla and the city. Both subregions are part of the Columbia Valley mega-AVA, which occupies the number-two slot behind California in overall U.S. grape production. This is a charmed site where four big rivers converge: the Yakima from the Cascades, the Snake and Columbia from the Rockies, and the Walla Walla from the Blue Mountains.

As you taste your way through Washington, it's worth remembering that, although the focus here is on red wines, you're not going to be getting the same rich, heavy wines you might be accustomed to from California, or even France, Spain, and Italy. Washington wines are rich and fruity but somewhat less oomphy than others based on Cabernet and Merlot.

But that's not a significant problem, because wine drinkers are increasingly interested in diversifying the styles of wine they drink. In a nutshell, this is the secret to both Washington and Oregon's success: They've provided

The Zephyr Ridge vineyard at Hogue cellars, where a family gamble paid off in the form of well-received wines.

[BASE CAMP]

By plane, Seattle-Tacoma International Airport is a Pacific Northwest hub that is serviced by many carriers. Then, by car, wine-country visitors can cross the Cascade Mountains on Interstate 90, a highway that covers the roughly three-hour drive southeast from Seattle. In Walla Walla, **STRAWBERRY CANYON LODGE** (9052 Mill Creek Rd., 509-529-5288, above) should appeal to the avid fisherman, both with its "roughing it" aesthetic and its secluded location (but don't miss out on the hot tub!). B&B lovers may want to check out the **INN AT BLACKBERRY CREEK** (1126 Pleasant St., 509-522-5233), a renovated 1912 farmhouse in the middle of wine country. Rooms are named for French Impressionist painters.

an alternative to the commonly accepted contemporary American style, which is "large and in charge." It's also important that Washington has supplied connoisseurs with a viable Cabernet alternative. One of the things that has held back quality-centric regions such as New York's Finger Lakes is the inability to market their red wines despite a world bent on red-wine consumption. That Washington produces reds that can ably compete with California's bodes well for the future of American regional winemaking.

And don't overlook Washington's sparkling wines (sparkling wines are something of a secret weapon for wineries outside California, as cooler growing conditions tend to favor this style). Chateau Ste Michelle produces a terrifically reliable bubbly that's available all over the country. It's worth tracking down (and it's not that hard to do it). Chateau Ste. Michelle is part of the gigantic Stimson Lane Group, which dominates the Washington wine industry.

SIPPIN' IN SEATTLE

Just as you shouldn't visit Oregon without checking out Portland, you've got to reserve a few days to check out Seattle if you're going to Washington. After all, it's the home of Boeing and the birthplace of grunge. For the wine-and-food lover, Seattle is a bonanza: a food-crazed city, jammed with upwardly mobile technology workers who like to eat. However, none of it comes off as intimidating or snobby; much of Washington's wine country still preserves its down-home quality. As you might imagine, fresh fish is

an important part of the local diet in these parts. Keep an eye out for sushi, a beloved foodstuff in Seattle.

There is a wine region within striking distance of Seattle: the Puget Sound region. However, because it's on the coastal side of the Cascade range, it tends to be pretty rainy (hence, Seattle's soggy reputation), although its climate varies far less than, say, that of the Yakima Valley. Plus, since the rain comes mostly in winter months, it doesn't have a detrimental effect on the vines.

Sheltered from the Pacific by the majestic Olympic Mountains, the picturesque Bainbridge and Whidbey Islands offer a lovely weekend retreat from the city. Wines here tend toward a more Germanic style of crispness and lightness.

If you decide to give Puget wines a shot, you have one notable recourse should you overindulge: Seattle is, of course, the home of Starbucks and something of a mecca for coffee fanatics. The original location is on Pike Place. Believe me, a nice double espresso both before and after a day of tasting can be a lifesaver.

TASTING TRAIL

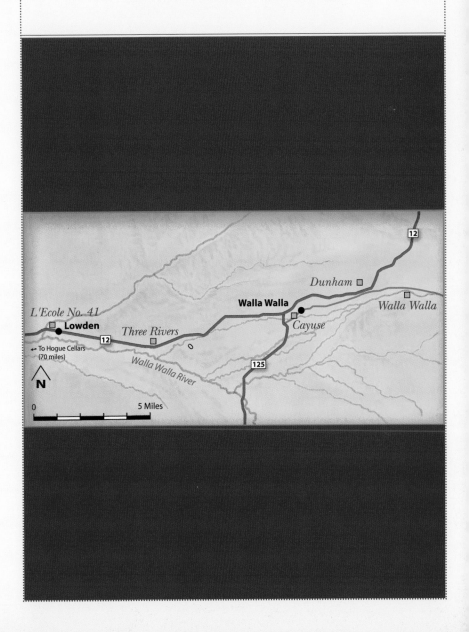

~⊙ Working the vineyard rows at the Armada vineyard, part of the Cayuse winery.

CAYUSE VINEYARDS

A Frenchman in the Pacific Northwest? Believe it. The French are unusually intrigued by what's happening in the American rain belt. Christophe Baron is originally from Champagne, but after a visit to Washington in the mid-1990s, he was won over and moved there. In the words of his PR: "While visiting the Walla Walla Valley in 1996, Christophe spotted a plot of land that had been plowed up to reveal acres of softball-sized stones. He became ridiculously excited. This stony soil, this terroir, was just like that of some of the most prestigious French appellations!" The difficult ground would stress the grapevines, making them produce more mature, concentrated fruit. Baron had found a new home. Why are stones such a big deal? Two reasons: They do indeed force grapevines to struggle for survival, thus putting more precious resources into fruit rather than leaves. Also, stony soil gathers heat during the day and then radiates it back to the vines at night. This makes for a longer, effective ripening period. Baron's wines are among the most esoteric in Washington. Some are available only by mailing list.

17 EAST MAIN ST.
WALLA WALLA, WA 99362
509-526-0686
WWW.CAYUSEVINEYARDS.COM

DUNHAM CELLARS

Dunham Cellars is located in an old airport hangar (note the Boeing address), and you could conceivably drop by this ten-year-old superachieving winery by Cessna. A very basic setup, not at all a tasting-room-cum-visitor-center extravaganza. And that's just the way they like it. At Dunham, wine takes precedence over decor. Cofounder Mike Dunham's son, Eric, is the winemaker. His '97 Cabernet Sauvignon put the winery on the map, and it's been onward and upward ever since. As with many wineries in the Pacific Northwest, Dunham participates in annual open houses, which are a great way to meet the owners and winemakers when they're in their glory, and when the Washington weather is cooperating.

150 EAST BOEING AVE.
WALLA WALLA, WA 99362
509-529-4685
WWW.DUNHAMCELLARS.COM

Cayuse's Cailloux vineyard, which is named, like the Cayuse Indians, after the French word for "rocks."

L'ECOLE NO. 41

Based out of a historic school from 1915, L'Ecole No. 41 is one of the Washington wine industry's leaders (it's been around since 1983). This is just a great place to taste wine and a great place to get an introduction to what Washington can do with classic French grapes. Everything in the tasting room has that old-elementary-school solidity, right down to the restored chalkboards, where visitors can leave messages next to wine prices. Owners Marty and Megan Clubb (Martin is the winemaker) do a great job with their wines, especially the Cabernet Sauvignon. Anyone looking for a true Bordeaux-style American wine should sample it.

41 LOWDEN SCHOOL RD.
LOWDEN, WA 99360
509-525-0940
WWW.LECOLE.COM

HOGUE CELLARS

If you have ever encountered a Washington wine, chances are it came from Hogue Cellars. Not only is it among Washington State's oldest premium wineries, it also has achieved excellent distribution outside its home market. Gary Hogue is one half of the two-brother team that founded Hogue Cellars. He is also one of those personalities that every winemaking region seems to need: a powerbroker. Hogue is a leader, a guy who can see around corners and explore new possibilities. He knows that for a winery to succeed in America, it needs broad exposure. This he has managed, with Hogue Cellars' white wines, mainly Rieslings. But Hogue is also coming on strong in reds. Its fifteen hundred acres allow for a large range of more than eight varieties of grapes and labels, from the everyday to the special reserve. Some folks in the wine press tend to think of Hogue as the Gallo of Washington wine, which is sort of true. There is an industrial-strength vibe to both the tasting room and the production facility. However, Hogue is and always has been a good, affordable Washington wine label to bet on.

2800 LEE RD.
PROSSER, WA 99350
509-786-4557
WWW.HOGUECELLARS.COM

~~⌇ *OPPOSITE:* L'Ecole No. 41 Winery in what used to be called Frenchtown, taking its name from the French settlers that came to the area in the nineteenth century.

~~⌇ *RIGHT:* Rows of vines at Hogue's Zephyr Ridge Vineyards.

THREE RIVERS WINERY

This is a good-sized facility, with a soaring, four-thousand-square-foot tasting room.
It's all pretty new, an indication of how the Washington wine business has boomed in
recent years (the tasting room and new production facility were completed in 1999).
The idea is to create, as the winery puts it, a destination experience. This includes
wonderful wines, as well as concerts at the winery's outdoor theater. If you're traveling in a pack, you might want to check out the on-site hospitality suite, which is available for a variety of events, from weddings to corporate outings.

5641 W. HWY 12
WALLA WALLA, WA 99362
509-526-WINE
WWW.THREERIVERSWINERY.COM

~∿⊗ Walla Walla Vintners, where the
owners produce quality wines
yet still keep their day jobs,
unrelated to winemaking.

WALLA WALLA VINTNERS

This winery is housed in a barnlike structure, with barrels stacked outside. Another recent venture (1995), the place is run by Myles Anderson and Gordon Venneri, a pair of home winemakers who decided to up the stakes on their hobby. So far, so good. Their touch with Bordeaux varietals—Cabernet Sauvignon, Merlot, and Cabernet Franc—seems sure. At least according to *Wine Spectator*, the world's largest-circulation wine magazine. Wine critic Harvey Steiman has awarded several Walla Walla bottlings prestigious 90-point scores (once a winery starts scoring in the 90s, it can say it has succeeded in raising its game to international levels.) This winery isn't open every day, so be sure to check or call ahead. As you might expect, the objective here is not to have tourists. However, if you make the effort, you will probably be rewarded with the personal touch.

225 VINEYARD LN.
WALLA WALLA, WA 99362
509-525-4724
WWW.WALLAWALLAVINTNERS.COM

*L*abels to look for

◎ THREE RIVERS COLUMBIA VALLEY CABERNET SAUVIGNON
A very satisfying intro to what many critics believe is Washington's secret weapon: Subtle and complex Cabs that stand in opposition to the monster reds of California and Australia.

◎ HOGUE GEWÜRZTRAMINER
Gewürz is all about spice, and this one—from one of Washington's largest and best-known producers—is always a safe bet.

◎ HOGUE JOHANNISBERG RIESLING
Hogue started out as a Riesling producer and remains true to the varietal in this bottling. Very representative of what European whites can be, in the hands of Washington vintners—incorporating flavors from lemon to coconut.

◎ L'ECOLE NO. 41 SEVEN HILLS VINEYARD MERLOT
It can be easy to get seduced by Washington Cabs, but the Merlots are pretty good, too. This rich, chocolate-tinged version is a solid example.

◎ WALLA WALLA VINTNERS COLUMBIA VALLEY CABERNET SAUVIGNON
Washington has made waves with its Bordeaux-style reds. This limited-production Cab is a good example. Delicious, without being syrupy or overly alcoholic.

◎ CAYUSE VINEYARDS CAILLOUX SYRAH
Winemaker Christophe Baron, a relocated Frenchman, has an affection for the rocky landscape of the Rhône. Given that *cailloux* means "stones," you can get what he's after with this wine. It's a Pacific Northwest take on a classic single-vineyard wine from the Rhône.

ℰ CHATEAU STE. MICHELLE BLANC DE BLANC

One of the best American sparkling wines you can drink for around $10. Gets my vote for bubbly to keep on hand at all times, and to drink at almost any time of day (a great sparkler to make mimosas with).

ℰ CHATEAU STE. MICHELLE CABERNET SAUVIGNON

Chateau Ste. Michelle maintains one of the most impressive lineups of premium wines in a state dedicated to premium wines. Over time, Cabernet has shown itself to be an impressive red wine in Washington State, and this one reveals why. It is both lushly fruity and smooth.

ℰ LEONETTI CABERNET SAUVIGNON

Leonetti has been setting a premium standard for Washington wines since 1978. This Cab routinely scores well with the wine press and provides a terrific example of what Washington Cabs, with their elegant flavors and lighter style, are all about.

ℰ LEONETTI MERLOT

Washington Merlots are often massively fruity and even aggressively chocolaty, but they're rarely thick or unctuous. Leonetti, a Washington leader in red wines, can be counted on to deliver a decent Merlot year after year.

ℰ COLUMBIA CREST CHARDONNAY

This well-known Washington winery does Cabernet and Riesling, but its Chardonnay offers a special opportunity to sample the Burgundian style that Washington goes after with the varietal.

ℰ SNOQUALMIE CABERNET SAUVIGNON

Whereas California and Australian Cabs can be overwhelmingly fruit-forward, Washington Cabs tend to be more balanced. Without getting into Snoqualmie's reserve bottlings (and parting with more dollars), this Cab shows how Washington winemakers have learned to judge the various elements in the king of grapes.

[AT A GLANCE: CALIFORNIA]

CENTRAL ROADS: Highway 29 (Napa), Highway 1 (Pacific Coast Highway)

TOWNS TO VISIT: San Francisco, Santa Cruz, Santa Barbara, Los Angeles, San Diego

LOCAL FLAVORS: Any kind of fresh produce, especially plums and figs.

AVERAGE BOTTLE PRICE: $10

BEST TIME TO VISIT: Year round.

WINERIES: 847

ACRES OF VINES: 500,000

YEARLY WINE PRODUCTION: More than half-a-billion gallons

TOP WINES:
Cabernet Sauvignon, Merlot, Syrah, Pinot Noir,
Zinfandel, Chardonnay, Sauvignon Blanc, sparkling wines

WEBSITE:
Info on California wine country abounds, but start with
the state's section on www.winespectator.com

THE BOTTOM LINE:
California produces ninety percent of all the wine made in the U.S.
Almost every type of wine produced in the world has
been tried out in California. Boundless ambition defines the state.

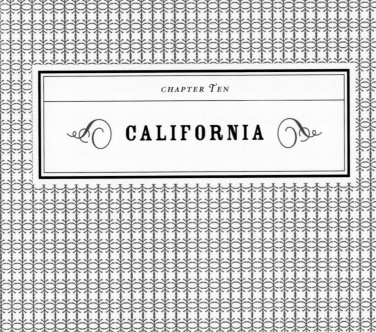

CHAPTER TEN

CALIFORNIA

THE ESSENCE OF AMERICAN WINE

California is more than just the most important American winemaking state. It's probably the most important winemaking region—or megaregion—in the world. It's often pointed out that California's economy is bigger than that of some countries. It wouldn't be too hard to argue that, in terms of global influence, the Golden State's wine industry is a bigger deal than France's or Italy's.

Why? Because although many of the techniques that now define high-quality international winemaking were pioneered in the Old World, California embraced these techniques and technologies before many others and pushed them to a new level, adding a healthy dose of aggressive marketing along the way.

Of course, there was always a substantial wine business in California, dating back all the way to the era of Spanish settlement. Prohibition set matters back somewhat in the 1920s, but after the amendment was repealed, California began to announce itself.

At first, the state took advantage of its almost preternaturally favorable growing conditions to crank out gallons of decent if unremarkable megawines. True, there were a few winemakers who labored for higher quality, but by and large, from the '30s to the '60s, California was the jug-wine capital of the universe.

This all changed in the '70s, when a daring band of revolutionaries began to realize that California—and specifically the wine regions of Napa and Sonoma, north of San Francisco—could produce wines that were competitive with the best the Old World, specifically France, had to offer. Over a decade, the premium wine business in California was developed, and we're still enjoying its spectacular success.

A bird's-eye view of the Neibaum-Coppola winery.

So, in a sense, California isn't really an American wine region; it's an *international* wine region. Accordingly, the wines it produces are really on a different level altogether from what almost every other American region puts on the market. For one thing, California wines are the bedrock upon which most U.S. wine stores build their stock. Enter any wine shop in any American city and the first wines you're likely to see are from California.

Also, California's wine output is enormous, dwarfing what even up-and-coming regions such as the Pacific Northwest crank out. California doesn't just produce one or two types of prominent wines. In addition to its marquee Cabernets and Chardonnays, it deals in everything from Viognier to Zinfandel. The vast Central Valley covers the bulk-wine scene, but the vineyards of the premium regions are so outrageously productive that California has, for several years now, been forced to endure gluts of both wine grapes and juice. Enterprising marketers have taken up this "excess capacity" and introduced dirt-cheap, pseudo-premium wines, like the "Two Buck Chuck" bottlings that are sold in California stores for $1.99 for a standard 750 ml bottle.

Other American regions can't compete with that kind of muscle, and it's crazy to expect them to try. This is why it makes the most sense for other regions to focus on styles of wine completely different from California's mainstays like Cabernet and Chardonnay. Economies of scale permit California to engage in very competitive pricing at the low

end, reserving the high end for only their most fabulous wines.

And in California—and especially in Napa Valley, the states premier AVA—the high end is dismayingly high. So-called "cult" wines, produced in minuscule quantities for a limited number of mailing-list customers, can command release prices that rival First Growth Bordeaux. Labels such as Screaming Eagle and Colgin have redefined the high-stakes wine game.

Meanwhile, prices continue to march steadily upward on great wines that are produced in larger quantities than the cult wines. This has some people worried, but it's just simple economics. As California's wine business has prospered, the cost of making prosperous California wines has been catapulted into the stratosphere. Take for instance the average price of an acre of land. In Texas wine country, you could find a deal for $5,000 an acre; in Napa the same plot would run you upwards of $200,000. Needless to say, if you hope to break into the premium-wine business, California is not necessarily the best place to start.

However, it's a wonderful place to learn. California currently operates the finest resource for the training of winemakers anywhere outside France. The University of California at Davis has trained and dispatched graduates to many up-and-coming U.S. wine regions. And even those vintners who don't have UC Davis degrees but who put in time working at the state's many, many premium wineries can head out to the provinces with the kind of experience

[DRIVING FORCES BEHIND CALIFORNIA WINE TODAY]

THE NEW PIONEERS

Novelist and wine writer Jay McInerney has called **HELEN TURLEY**, the taciturn mistress of the cult wine, a wine diva. He might be on to something. Certainly, Turley is one of the most famous winemakers in the world. Legendarily exacting and difficult to work with (it's her way or the hard way), she has led the charge to produce a distinctive, extremely powerful style of American red wine that some critics adore but others accuse of being over the top.

PAUL DRAPER is the gentle, cerebral soul behind Ridge, one of California's most reliably excellent wine labels. Draper has an interesting background for a winemaker—something out of a thriller by John le Carré. He worked for a while as a youth in Army intelligence in Europe. It was there that he got the wine bug, and it was good-bye to spooking for Uncle Sam.

RANDALL GRAHM combines several roles into one: winemaker, litterateur, philosopher, idealist, evangelist . . . well, you could go on and on about the proprietor of Bonny Doon. Grahm is sui generis in the California wine scene. Scratch that—he's sui generis in the world wine scene. Scratch that—he's just sui generis. There's nobody anywhere even remotely like Grahm. They broke the mold for his kind sometime in the last century.

ALEXIS SWANSON, the eldest of W. Clark Swanson Jr.'s three daughters, not only has a wine named after her—she makes sure that people buy it. As Swanson Vineyards' marketing manager, Alexis is a one-woman traveling promoter of her family's products. She is also something of a social figure, an always well-turned-out personality, and a woman whose photo not infrequently appears in magazines such as *W*.

GINA GALLO is the new face of Gallo, and not just in the magazine ads. Gina has taken the helm at this American winemaking giant's relatively new premium-wine venture, Gallo of Sonoma. The youthful Gallo represents the next generation of Gallos to produce wine in California, ensuring that the name not only lives on but continues to evolve.

In Napa, foodies should make a pilgrimage to **COPIA: THE AMERICAN CENTER FOR WINE, FOOD, AND THE ARTS** (500 First St., 888-51-COPIA, above). But they might want to eat at the famous **MUSTARDS GRILL** (7399 Hwy. 29, Yountville, 707-944-2424), where the local winemakers gather to gossip. Writer Jack London was an early literary exile in sunny California (he identified surfers before anyone knew what the sport was); in Sonoma, you can see the ruins of his "Wolf House" in the **JACK LONDON STATE HISTORIC PARK** (2400 London Ranch Rd., Glen Ellen, 707-938-5216). Two ways to take in the California wine country in style are by train and by…balloon. Yes, balloon. Slow, scenic balloon tours of Napa are offered by several local tour companies. Closer to earth, the **NAPA WINE TRAIN** takes a three-hour ride through the vineyards, offering passengers wine, lunch, and dinner (1275 McKinstry St., 707-253-2111).

that's impossible to come by, regardless of how many hours one spends laboring in the vineyards or the cellar.

THE BIRTH OF THE TASTING ROOM

There are at least a dozen California winemakers who can claim they helped put the state on the world wine-producing map. Gallo, Mondavi, Jackson, Phelps, Heitz — the list is a who's who of homegrown visionaries. Some have sadly departed. But their extraordinary legacy lives on. Perhaps their greatest achievement—outside the bottle—is the transformation of a sleepy farm town like Napa into a world-renowned tourist destination, with all the advantages and problems that involves. Given the climate, it's almost never a bad time to visit. However, from late summer on through the fall and in spring, Napa tends to get crowded. During the summer, daytime temperatures can really heat up, causing visitors to think twice about putting the top down on the rented convertible. The winter months—November, December, January, February—are generally a good bet for a more subdued scene (just don't assume you'll be able to get a reservation any easier at Thomas Keller's famous French Laundry restaurant).

Napa is significantly less down-home these days than many other wine regions (the price of runaway success). Most big-name wineries host concerts and tours, but they are of a highly professional nature. Hayrides through the vineyards are unusual. You can't just walk up and start a casual conversation with the winemaker here as you can in other regions. But what Napa lacks in homeyness it more than makes up for in architectural splendor and sheer scenic grandeur. All along Highway 29, on the valley floor, there are astounding edifices that house the country's best winemaking operations. From the Robert Mondavi winery, a Spanish-style trendsetter, to the old Inglenook mansion, a beautifully restored Victorian structure now owned by filmmaker Francis Ford Coppola, Napa doesn't lack for enthralling aesthetic spectacles.

You'll want to carry a fat wallet if you intend to taste wine in most of Napa's better-known wineries; they all charge a tasting fee, sometimes a steep one for their more highly coveted bottlings. My advice is to skip it and instead treat Napa's main drag as a sightseeing exercise, then drop in at one of the town's several well-regarded eateries (my favorite is Mustards Grill) and start with a flight for tasting, then share a full bottle with dinner in a more relaxing setting.

Obviously, California wine is about much, much more than Napa Valley. Nearby Sonoma is considered by many wine-country veterans to be a generally more laid-back scene. It offers better driving, with plenty of narrow country roads that wind in and out of leafy tree stands, and some straightaways. The mood in Sonoma isn't self-consciously anti-Napa, but the wineries here tend to be a lot less businesslike and a lot more like the unpretentious agricultural operations that, down deep, they really are.

If Sonoma is still too go-go for your tastes, there's always Mendocino, which has just about everything that

The Bacchus fountain at Clos Pegase winery.

Napa and Sonoma do in terms of wines and tasting rooms, but with plenty of alternative-culture types running the show. It's not quite Oregon in terms of its rebuttal of wine-country flash, but it's close.

Mendocino can be a little bare bones. For a similar vibe, check out the Monterey Peninsula. Monterey is famous for its world-class golf courses—Pebble Beach, Spyglass Hills—but it also boasts a fantastic wine culture. One thing you'll immediately notice is that, away from the storybook town of Carmel, much of the peninsula seems like a throwback to California in the 1970s, with a laid-back folkie sort of atmosphere governing the ranches and lodges that dot the landscape. In recent years, however, some more upscale elements have crept in. Case in point: Bernardus Lodge, which has taken the rural roadside lodge motif and jacked it up to world-class resort status, complete with a critic-friendly restaurant and a croquet green.

More adventurous budding oenophiles will want to check out Santa Cruz, on the other side of Monterey Bay from Carmel. This is the headquarters of the "Rhône Rangers," a band of cheerfully radical winemakers who have energetically worked to adapt Syrah to California. Two wineries to keep an eye out for are Bonny Doon, run by the erudite, unconventional Randall Grahm, and Ridge, overseen by Paul Draper, considered by many to be California's most knowledgeable and interesting vintner (he did a stint in Army intelligence before he decided to become a winemaker).

BEYOND NAPA AND INTO THE FUTURE

Too often we think of the regions around San Francisco as the center of gravity for California's wine industry. While it's true that Napa, Sonoma, and Monterey are pretty much the engine that pulls the American premium-wine train forward, there's plenty going on farther south in the wine country near Santa Barbara. Of particular interest here is the burgeoning Pinot Noir scene. Spend any time in California touring wine country, and you'll eventually hear the phrase "microclimate." Essentially, this refers to very localized climatic conditions that make the cultivation of certain varieties of premium wine grapes easier. In Napa, for example, hot days and cool nights, as well as the availability of both flat and mountainous vineyard sites, seem like an ideal combination for Cabernet Sauvignon. Sonoma's Russian River Valley, on the other hand, does great Chardonnay.

In the Santa Barbara area, a peculiar climatic tic yields terrific Pinot Noir. What happens is that mountain ranges essentially funnel cool, foggy air inland from the coast. This pattern acts as a sort of natural air conditioner, preventing the naturally hot and arid Southern California climate from cooking the moody Pinot Noir grape on its vines. The result: rich, fruity wines that don't suffer from the jammy aspects that can affect Pinot Noirs produced up above San Francisco, where, paradoxically, overall temperatures can run higher. They've done the seemingly impossible in Santa Barbara: They've taken this neurotic Burgundian grape and created wines of substance and power time after time. A remarkable achievement—at least until Pinot-philes pipe up. Here's the problem: California—because even its cooler regions tend to have a far more favorable wine-growing climate than most places in the world—makes Pinot that's almost too good. How can it be too good? It's so fruity, drinkable, and delicious that it lacks some of the sophistication that classic Pinot Noir is supposed to have. The vinoscenti tend to favor Oregon Pinots, which are more complex. Still, if you want to enjoy your Pinot, and if you don't suffer from snobby predilections, then California is a very safe bet.

Whether it's Pinot from Santa Barbara or Cab from Napa, one trend has been shaping the entire state's output lately—rising prices. California got slammed over the past few years on price as a grape glut developed and inventories piled up. The good news is that you should look for California wine prices to come down over the next decade, relative to where they were. With global competition, especially in the $7 to $10 range, heating up, California will have to bring its wines more into line with the international market to avoid losing its share to Europe and Australia. And eventually, other states will pull an Oregon and begin to undermine California's domination of the high end.

To keep its status as America's winemaking leader, California needs a new tactic; developing a new

[BASE CAMP]

In Napa, **THE SILVER ROSE INN AND SPA** offers the chance for harried travelers who have duked it out all day up and down Route 29 to relax and kick back. Located near Calistoga, the Inn has a total of twenty rooms. Guests can enjoy the putting green and tennis courts, as well as the usual range of spa options (351 Rosedale Rd., 800-995-9381). If quaint is your game, you might want to check out the **WINE COUNTRY INN** (1152 Lodi Ln., St. Helena, 707-963-7077), with its twenty-four rooms and five cottages, each custom-decorated with cozy wine-country staples such as poster beds and handmade quilts. Farther south, on the Monterey Peninsula, **BERNARDUS LODGE** offers an outstanding resort experience as well as easy access to the region's wineries (415 Carmel Valley Rd., Carmel Valley, 831-658-3550, above). And even farther down south, Santa Barbara boasts a spectacular coastline dubbed the "American Riviera," as well as a string of beachfront hotels and luxurious resorts.

"big" wine isn't going to work. Syrah was the last big wine and it has, by now, established itself pretty well. Everything else that's been tried lately—Sangiovese, Tempranillo—has been a qualified failure. Instead, California winemakers are heading toward something else. They have discovered terroir in a big way. And despite the protests of some—that the state doesn't actually have any terroir—winemakers are currently working to refine their understanding of the places where their grapes actually grow. In the future, this will be what you should look for in California wines: more information about specific vineyards on the labels, along with an increasing number of single-vineyard bottlings.

But the best way to divine California's future is to get out there and start tasting. For true wine-country touring fanatics, California provides one of the best ways to take in everything the state has to offer: Highway 1, the Pacific Coast Highway, which runs along the coast for hundreds of miles, from San Diego to San Francisco, and points north. This is arguably the best drive in the world. North to south, the Pacific looms off your right shoulder, a vast, imposing presence. And the scenery changes constantly, from the mountainous, evergreen grandeur of Big Sur to the flattened-out minimalism of the landscape of the central coast. You'll know you're nearing Santa Barbara when you catch sight of the oil platform twinkling in the distance. The overall impression you get from this experience is one of largeness: California is huge. And so is its wine industry.

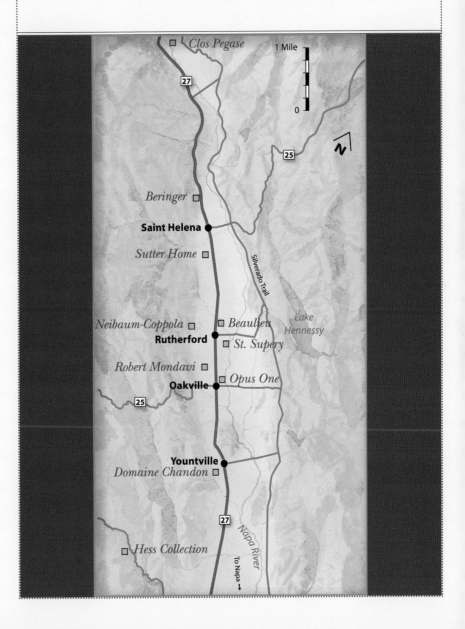

THE NAPA VALLEY

TASTING TRAIL

Clos Pegase

27

25

1 Mile

0

Beringer

Saint Helena

Sutter Home

Silverado Trail

Lake Hennessy

Neibaum-Coppola   Beaulieu

Rutherford   St. Supery

Robert Mondavi

Opus One

Oakville

25

Yountville

Domaine Chandon

27

Napa River

To Napa →

Hess Collection

SAN FRANCISCO

Beringer's Rhine House.

BEAULIEU VINEYARD

Here's what you need to know about this storied winery: It's where André Tchelistcheff, the most important winemaker in the history of American wine, did his earliest and best work, as an escapee from escalating European fascism in the late 1930s. California had only recently emerged from Prohibition, and Georges de Latour, Beaulieu's owner, brought Tchelistcheff to California from Paris, where he had been working at a university. Tchelistcheff recognized immediately that he had a unique opportunity in Napa. He could see the future and set about crafting it, in the form of wines. His present-day successor, Joel Aiken, has put his own stamp on BV, creating a line of special winemaker's products, from barbecue sauce to marinades, that are sold in the winery's tasting room. The tasting room is housed in the winery's original building, a simple, welcoming stone edifice that George de Latour constructed. Beaulieu's cellar recently suffered from a bout of "cellar taint," but the owners have taken steps to solve the problem. Regardless, George de Latour Private Reserve remains one of the greatest—perhaps the greatest—Napa Cabernets. Why is it such a big deal? Because library vintages date back to the 1930s, demonstrating a track record for age worthiness that rivals French Bordeaux.

1960 ST. HELENA HWY.
RUTHERFORD, CA 94573
707-963-2411
WWW.BVWINES.COM

Beaulieu Vineyard, where George de Latour overcame the tricky obstacle of the vine-killer *phylloxera* by using imported rootstock.

BERINGER VINEYARDS

Founded in 1876, Beringer showcases Napa's Germanic side. The historic Rhine House, where you'll find the multifloor tasting rooms, is straight out of a Teutonic fantasy. There are stained-glass windows, heavy wood wainscoting, and a pair of suits of armor believed to represent, according to the winery, the founding brothers, Frederick and Jacob, who arrived in Napa from Germany with wine on their minds. One might expect Riesling from such a place, but Cabernet and Chardonnay—as well as a delicious (believe it or not) blush wine—are the real story. Skillfully produced by Beringer's winemaker, Ed Sbragia, Beringer's wines

2000 MAIN ST.
ST. HELENA, CA 94574
707-963-4812
WWW.BERINGER.COM

are Napa classics. In addition to tastings and tours of the property, the Beringer Master Series on food and wine is worth investigating. More and more wineries are beginning to offer these comprehensive courses on Napa food and wine, often featuring the region's star chefs. In Beringer's case, the lineup reads like a who's who of California culinary talent.

The arched entryway to Domaine Chandon.

DOMAINE CHANDON

This California outpost of one of France's major Champagne producers, Moët et Chandon, is a must-see. The winery is architecturally a mellow, quiet affair, its gentle curves and woodsy palette striving to blend into the landscape. Sculptures can be seen scattered throughout the grounds. Although the winery produces still wines, its reputation rests on sparkling wines (according to the French tradition, only sparklers from Champagne can be called "Champagne"). A major reason to schedule a visit to Domaine Chandon in advance is to experience the winery's award-winning restaurant, whose menu features an ever-changing lineup of seasonal California cuisine.

ONE CALIFORNIA DR.
YOUNTVILLE, CA 94599
707-944-2280
WWW.CHANDON.COM

ROBERT MONDAVI WINERY

This was California's first truly modern winery, founded in 1966 by Robert Mondavi, perhaps the most significant living American vintner. Mondavi has explained that he hoped creating a dramatic, architecturally appealing winery would attract visitors. How he has succeeded in that ambition! This is probably Napa's *most* visited winery. It has grown beyond its original contemporary Spanish-style structure—well known from the winery's labels—to a small campus of buildings, all themed around Mondavi's passion: that wine and the enjoyment of life cannot be separated. If you're interested in every nuance of his storied career, pick up his autobiography, *Harvests of Joy*. Mondavi was instrumental in steering Napa Valley into its current position as the preeminent winemaking region in America—and as one of the three or four great winemaking regions of the world. This winery is among the easier Napa institutions to deal with. It is roomy, offering plenty of tasting rooms to explore and ample grounds to walk around. As popular as it is, it's still a contemplative place where you can pause and consider how far California winemaking has come since the '60s, when this winery was considered revolutionary. Regular tours of the facility offer tremendous insight into Robert Mondavi, his family, and the wine industry of California, and, of course, they serve as a nice introduction to one of the best lineups of premium wines to be found anywhere. Now an éminence grise in Napa, Mondavi has every excuse to slow down and allow his sons and daughter to assume his mantle. To a degree, he has. But his energy remains boundless for a man heading toward his eighth decade. Lately, he has taken an interest in expanding the company's reach into other up-and-coming international wine regions, such as southern France and Italy.

7801 ST. HELENA HWY.
OAKVILLE, CA 94562
888-766-6328
WWW.ROBERTMONDAVIWINERY.COM

The mission-style Robert Mondavi Winery, which paved the way not only for the Mondavi empire but for the Napa wine industry.

The vineyards of Opus One winery.

OPUS ONE

There's old Napa and there's new Napa, and then there's Opus One, which is sui generis. Across the street from the Robert Mondavi Winery, this is the physical expression of a collaboration between Robert Mondavi and the late Baron Philippe de Rothschild of Bordeaux's legendary Château Mouton Rothschild. The winery was opened in 1991, but the meeting of these two wine-world titans actually took place several decades earlier. Rothschild had passed away by the time the Opus One winery was finished, but Mondavi was certainly around to witness the fulfillment of a lifelong dream: to bring the greatest wines of Europe and America together. The entire design of the rather striking facility rests on one principle: to produce wines as delicately as possible. This was the winery that made "gravity flow" famous. The juice from crushed grapes is never pumped mechanically into fermentation tanks; instead, everything has been laid out so that juice can move through the winemaking process aided only by gravity. Ultimately, this makes for extremely slo-mo bottling of wines, which are typically released three years after the grapes are picked. Is it worth it? It's not entirely clear at this point, as there have been a limited number of vintages. But the product seems to have an excellent combination of French and American virtues.

7900 ST. HELENA HWY.
OAKVILLE, CA 94562
707-944-9442
WWW.OPUSONEWINES.COM

NIEBAUM-COPPOLA

Director Francis Ford Coppola deserves a lot of credit for his *Godfather* trilogy of movies and also for *Apocalypse Now,* but to wine lovers, his greatest achievement was to save the old Inglenook estate from certain destruction. Inglenook was America's original great winery—long before anyone had even thought that California might be able to make world-class wines. The original winery was founded in 1880 by a Norwegian sea captain, Gustave Niebaum. Over the decades, Inglenook gradually set a standard for California winemaking. Of course, the word never really got out, and over time Inglenook's accomplish-

1991 ST. HELENA HWY.
RUTHERFORD, CA 94573
800-782-4266
WWW.NIEBAUM-COPPOLA.COM

ments faded. Well ahead of the California wine boom, Coppola bought a chunk
of the estate in the mid-1970s and not long after began to produce wine under the
Rubicon label. Gradually, Coppola acquired the rest of the property, including
the ornate château that Gustave Niebaum had constructed decades before. In
maverick fashion, Coppola bought the home so that he wouldn't have to live and
work anywhere near Hollywood. The enterprising, idiosyncratic, and iconoclas-
tic thrust of his story is emblematic of the whole sensibility of the American
wine boom. Adding a layer, of course, is the parallel fact that no one took
California wine, even from an old and established estate, very seriously in the
'70s. Obviously, Coppola was on to something, although he claims that he doesn't
know that much about wine. What does it matter? He gave the professionals
more or less free reign to expand the winemaking program, and he has become a
sort of wine-world mogul, assembling a varied lineup of wines under his labels
that are all leaders in their class, from inexpensive, everyday quaffers in the
"Coppola Presents" range to the top-of-the-pile Rubicon. Now, Niebaum-
Coppola is an essential stop on the Napa wine trail.

ST. SUPÉRY VINEYARDS AND WINERY

This is where you'll find the Wine Discovery Center, an interactive winemaking facility, as well as an art gallery and a historic Napa home that forms the centerpiece of the winery. If all that sounds a little like visiting Napa's version of a science-and-industry museum . . . well, Napa likes to get visitors involved in its story. St. Supéry, which was founded by a Frenchman, is more enthusiastic about doing this than most other wineries. In the fall, for example, a Harvest Adventure program is offered (for $250). Visitors stay at the estate, participate in the harvest experience (including learning how to make wines in the cellar), and get to enjoy some superb cuisine, courtesy of the winery's chef. Now, an American regional wine enthusiast could argue that this can all be had for free at countless locales outside Napa, where harvest time is usually also a time when wineries are happy to accept the services of volunteers. However, that's not the point. In Napa, most of the grapes are actually picked by serious, trained, well-compensated pickers. So St. Supéry's program is, in the end, worth the expenditure, as it gives visitors a glimpse of what the wine life in Napa is really all about. If you really get hooked, St. Supéry offers another program, "Grow Your Own," which enables people interested in viticulture to cultivate their very own Cabernet Sauvignon vine on the estate.

8440 ST. HELENA HWY.
RUTHERFORD, CA 94573
800-942-0809
WWW.STSUPERY.COM

An event on the lawn of St. Supery.

~~⊗ Clos Pegase, a winery with a
keen sense of the mythology
and traditions of winemaking.

CLOS PEGASE

There are many ways to get noticed in the California wine scene. You can produce outstanding wines in small quantities. You can build an architecturally stunning winery and attract visitors to its impressive confines. Or you can combine
both those gambits, as Clos Pegase has done. Owner Jan Shrem, who made his
fortune in Japan as a publisher, proved he had an eye for talent when he decided
to undertake a winery venture. First, he employed the services of André
Tchelistcheff, a Russian émigré regarded by many as the finest winemaker in
Napa's history. Then, once it came time to build a new winery, he hired architect
Michael Graves to build the facility. Graves delivered a "temple among the
vines," (as they like to say at Clos Pegase), a Mediterranean-style terra-cotta mas-
terpiece that houses all of Clos Pegase's winemaking operations, but that also
acts as a gallery for Shrem's art collection. Simply put, this winery is a wonderful
place to wander around, in addition to tasting wine. The wines of Clos Pegase are
fairly impressive. The focus here, in typical Napa fashion, is on Bordeaux
varietals—Cabernet and Merlot—and Chardonnay.

1060 DUNAWEAL LN.
CALISTOGA, CA 94515
707-942-4981
WWW.CLOSPEGASE.COM

THE HESS COLLECTION

The Hess Collection isn't just a collection of great wines; it's a collection of great art. The extensive gallery displays a portion of the artwork collected by Donald Hess over the course of thirty years. Interestingly, before Hess took over the property, it was owned and operated by the famous Christian Brothers religious order, which gained renown for its winemaking in the days before the big California wine boom. (Actually, the history of the property, situated in the Mount Veeder area, goes back to the nineteenth century.) Nowadays, the name of the game here—besides contemporary paintings from the likes of Francis Bacon—is, as one might expect, Cabernet and Chardonnay.

4411 REDWOOD RD.

NAPA, CA 94558

707-255-1144

WWW.HESSCOLLECTION.COM

ABOVE: Hess Collection vineyards on the slopes of Mount Veder.

SUTTER HOME WINERY

Sutter Home is now a label that operates under the Trinchero Family Estates' umbrella (the Trinchero family has owned Sutter Home since 1947). The Sutter Home Winery is located right on the main drag in Napa and is thus worth a stop. For many visitors, a taste of a Sutter Home wine will not be a new experience, given that the wines are widely distributed. The wines made here—and there are many different types produced—are well known all across the country. They are what is now referred to as "fighting varietals," or varietally labeled wines that are priced reasonably (usually under $10), compared to other "premium" California wines. The saga of the family that built the winery into the megabrand that it is today can be found in the book *Harvesting the Dream: Rags-to-Riches Tale of the Sutter Home Winery.*

277 ST. HELENA HWY.

ST. HELENA, CA 94574

707-963-3104

WWW.SUTTERHOME.COM

The Sutter Home winery, which practices environmentally sound winemaking and even uses bottles made from recycled glass.

*L*ABELS TO LOOK FOR

 ROBERT MONDAVI CABERNET SAUVIGNON RESERVE

This Cab has always set a standard for contemporary California wine. Still not stratospherically expensive, it delivers everything that Napa Cab lovers adore and have come to expect from the region: rich, dark fruit flavors, firm tannins, delicious oak, and abundant underlying structure. Twenty-year-old vintages are still drinking beautifully. If you've ever had any doubts about the greatness of American red wine relative to French Bordeaux, this label should more than reassure you.

 PEPPERWOOD GROVE PINOT NOIR

Cheap, cheerful, and good. Any bottling from this American negociant—owned and operated by Don Sebastiani, a scion of one of California's great wine families—is a splendid value. The Pinot Noir is a sub-$10 marvel. Not sophisticated, but a nice everyday Pinot.

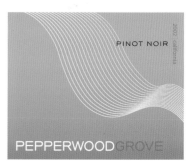

 BEAULIEU VINEYARD GEORGES DE LATOUR PRIVATE
   RESERVE CABERNET SAUVIGNON

This wine has been produced in Napa for sixty years, and it's always a mouthful: ripe, delicious flavors of black currant and chocolate, with plenty of spice and oak backing things up. Plenty of tannin as well to ensure a long life. There are still examples around from the 1930s. Possibly the closest Napa has come to producing an authentic rival to Bordeaux.

⟲ BONNY DOON/CA' DEL SOLO BIG HOUSE RED

Bring on the screw cap! Randall Grahm is the madcap personality behind this wine, which is perfect for pizza (according to no less an authority than Robert Parker!). Recently, Grahm lost the cork, which was already made from plastic, and replaced it with a screw cap. The upshot is that this always reliable, always robust red blend can now be assumed to be spoilage proof. There's also an equally delicious, also foolproof white version, Big House White.

⟲ NIEBAUM-COPPOLA ROSSO

This is Frances Ford Coppola's basic red bottling, and it's absolutely terrific, year after year. At roughly $12, it is not going to compete with the winery's top-of-the-line Rubicon, but that's okay. Full-bodied, loaded with blackberry and oak flavors, it makes a wonderful wine with simple pasta dishes.

⟲ CLOS PEGASE HOMMAGE CABERNET SAUVIGNON

This is Clos Pegase's version of Mouton Rothschild: a brilliant and powerful Cabernet-based wine that features commissioned art on the label. This textbook Napa reserve Cab, loaded with black currant flavors and chewy tannins—as well as no shortage of toasty oak—is a California standard-bearer. You'll pay to drink it, though; the retail price hovers around $75.

⟲ OPUS ONE

A powerful, complex Cabernet-based wine that, on release, set a record for a California red wine in terms of sale price. It continues to be hot on the auction block and, of course, in continuing releases. What's remarkable about this wine is that it is held back from market even longer than many First Growth Bordeaux (thirty-six months).

⟲ BERINGER PRIVATE RESERVE NAPA VALLEY CABERNET SAUVIGNON

Always a good bet among California Cabernets. The 1997 vintage was magnificent, but also worth looking for are 1994 and 1999. A typically rich and powerful mass of black fruit and layered complexity.

ⓒ SUTTER HOME WHITE ZINFANDEL

California's answer to French rosé—and the original American pink wine. Say what you will about white Zin, nothing goes down better with fresh mozzarella on a warm summer afternoon. It's been so long—thirty years—since this wine took America by storm that people have forgotten how interesting it is.

ⓒ STAG'S LEAP CASK 23 ESTATE CABERNET SAUVIGNON

Stag's Leap was the red wine that beat out the French in the Judgment of Paris in 1976 (see Château Montelena Napa Valley Chardonnay for one of the whites that did likewise). Never cheap, bottles now retail upward of $150.

ⓒ GALLO OF SONOMA CHARDONNAY

Several years back, Gallo—California's most famous bulk-wine producer—decided to burnish its image by entering the premium-wine market. The Gallo of Sonoma label is the result. This Chardonnay, which usually sells for around $12, is an affordable summary of what California Chard is all about: The flavors are rich, borderline tropical, and there's a nice buttery texture to go along with the toasty oak.

ⓒ CHARLES SHAW CABERNET SAUVIGNON

If *Wine Spectator* had been feeling frisky in 2003, they would have named this wine, which retails for $1.99 at Trader Joe's stores in California, its Wine of the Year. "Two Buck Chuck" certainly touched off a flurry of commentary when it was released—and when shoppers started buying it by the caseload. This is the label that saved California from its worrying grape glut, by essentially creating a fire sale for grapes and juice that had accumulated in the aftermath of the '90s wine boom.

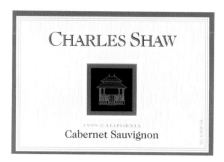

ⓒ DOMAINE CHANDON BRUT CLASSIC

This sparkler combines Chardonnay, Pinot Meunièr, Pinot Noir—and plenty of bubbles. The result is an expression of California's take on Champagne, classically rendered. To improve the overall quality of the bottling, a percentage of Chandon reserve wine from good vintages is blended in. This means that the wine can't carry a vintage date, but who cares? It's creamy, elegant, and delicious.

ⓒ ST. SUPÉRY CABERNET SAUVIGNON

Another outstanding Napa Cab, showcasing the signature regional flavors of vanilla and currants. In the matter of vintage, 1997 and 1994 are worth tracking down to drink now.

ⓒ THE HESS COLLECTION RESERVE CABERNET SAUVIGNON

This is Hess's preeminent wine, one that's usually worth buying and holding for a while until the rugged tannins mellow sufficiently and powerful dark berry flavors begin to mature. How long should you wait? Try at least a decade.

ⓒ SWANSON VINEYARDS ALEXIS

A beautiful California Cab from a boutique winery that maintains an obsessive focus on quality. "Alexis" is Alexis Swanson, one of the principals at the winery (her father started the operation) and a youthful force in California wine.

GLOSSARY

AVA: American Viticultural Area. This is a geographical distinction that's established by the U.S. government's Bureau of Alcohol, Tobacco, and Firearms. An AVA serves as an announcement that a winemaking region has gotten its act together and should be recognized as doing viticulture—meaning growing grapes to produce wine, a regulated beverage—not just farming. It's a big deal.

ACIDITY: All wines are acidic to some degree or another. A skillful winemaker balances acidity with tannin and fruitiness to create a harmonious composition. Too much acid throws the wine out of balance. But a wine with properly regulated acidity will have a refreshing aspect that, even in a robust vintage, brings a taster back for another sip.

BARRELS: Almost invariably made of oak. Coopers—or barrel makers—can, however, customize barrels extensively. Some winemakers go so far as to travel to France and visit forests to pick out the trees that will eventually become their barrels. The main tool that the barrel-maker has at his disposal is fire: The flavors that a barrel imparts to a wine can be greatly influenced by the degree of toast that is imparted by a skilled cooper. Toasting of barrels is very low-tech; coopers light a fire and expose the interior for prescribed amounts of time, thereby producing a barrel with "light," "medium," or "heavy" toast. A barrel can be used once or many times, depending on what the winemaker wants. Wines that are neither fermented nor aged in oak are said in Australia to be "unwooded." In America, they're sometimes said to be "unoaked."

BOUQUET: An old-fashioned term that tries to define what an older wine smells like. Distinct from "nose" or "aroma," both of which address the way younger wines smell. In short, if you're talking bouquet, you're attempting to judge a wine that has some age on it.

CORKED: The term for a wine tainted by TCA (2,4,6 trichloroanisole), a chemical compound that essentially destroys a wine's freshness. Corked wines smell musty and taste deflated. Some producers have sought to eliminate the problem—which afflicts one out of every twenty-four bottles—by moving to synthetic corks. Quite often it's not the cork that's the problem when something tastes "off," however. It's your wine glass, which can pick up all sorts of aromas from soap or the cabinet it's stored in. It's a good idea to rinse your glasses, either with water or wine, before using them.

CULT WINE: A California wine, generally a Cabernet Sauvignon–based bottling, produced in tiny quantities, often by a celebrity winemaker, and sold at phenomenally high prices to an exclusive clientele. These wines are distributed almost exclusively by mailing lists, and the lists are profoundly difficult to get on. Big names are Colgin, Bryant Family, and Screaming Eagle. The wines themselves are rich, heavy, and dense. Critics maintain that they are all for show and will not age as well as the top Bordeaux they are meant to compete with.

DRY: The vast majority of wines produced worldwide are referred to as "dry," meaning that most of their original sugar has been transformed into alcohol. Some important wines, however—notably German Riesling—do not have all their sugar fermented out. These wines are sometimes referred to as being "off dry." The sugar that doesn't get fermented is called "residual" sugar.

ESTATE-GROWN: If grapes that go into a winery's wines are entirely cultivated in vineyards owned by the estate, they are called "estate grown." This is generally a mark of pride, as the winery is in both the grape-farming and winemaking business. The practice allows the winery to control the quality of its grapes. However, just because a winery doesn't make its wine from estate-grown grapes, it doesn't mean the wines are inferior. Often, a winemaker will prefer to "source" grapes from vineyards he doesn't own.

FERMENTATION: The chemical process by which yeast transforms sugar into alcohol. All wines go through it. One of the byproducts of fermentation is carbon dioxide. Champagne and sparkling wine are allowed to undergo a second fermentation in the bottle, which generates the bubbles.

FLIGHT: Visit a tasting room and you will often be offered one of these. It is a lineup of wines, usually arranged from whites through reds and then sweet wines, in ascending order of price and quality. A flight will usually involve 5–10 wines.

ICE WINE: There are two ways to produce ice wine. The authentic way allows the grapes to hang on their vines until late in the year (or early the next), waiting for winter to strike and freeze the grapes. This concentrates the grapes' flavors, leading to an intense, sweet wine of considerable nuance and complexity. Ice wines are almost exclusively produced in northerly wine regions (such as upstate New York and Canada), where grapes that would otherwise taste terrible as wine benefit from the freezing process. The alternative way to make ice wine is to freeze the grapes artificially. This can also yield ice wines that are very good. Bonny Doon, in California, makes one it calls vin de glacier.

MICROCLIMATE: Most quality wine-growing regions benefit from this. A microclimate is a condition in which the local climate is literally distinct from its surroundings. For example, it may have very hot days and very cool nights (ideal for wine-grape cultivation). It may rain only one month out of the year. Or it may benefit from maritime cooling effects, which regulate the temperature. For example, there are areas in southern California that can actually be cooler than northern California due to chilly coastal fog that is funneled inland from the sea through canyons.

OAK: Often, but not always, wines spend some time in oak barrels before they're bottled. There are a variety of reasons for this. Sometimes, winemakers want the oak to add depth and complexity to the wine. Other times, they just want the wine to pick up particular oak flavors, such as vanilla or toast. Less-expensive wines will sometimes be dosed with oak chips or staves for a little extra flavor kick. But for winemakers willing to spend the money, there are several types of barrels that predominate. French oak tends to be softer and less obtrusive. American oak is more aggressive but popular because it can deliver a blast of charry flavor. Slovenian oak is something of a cult preoccupation, and it has adherents who see it as a third way, between pricey French and heavy-duty American oak.

PREMIUM: In America, a "premium" wine is defined as anything that costs more than $7. In practice, the term applies to varietal wines (Chardonnay, Merlot) that are sold under the pretense that they are a quality product, a few notches above bulk wines or jug wines. Premium wines are generally sold in 750ml bottles.

PROPRIETARY: Wines that aren't varietally labeled, but that instead have a singular name. Opus One, a collaboration between the Mondavis of Napa and the Rothschilds of Bordeaux, is perhaps the most famous example. It is a Cabernet Sauvignon-based wine that isn't labeled as such.

QUAFFER: Also known as "plonk," an unsophisticated wine meant to go down easy. Nothing fancy, a chugalug wine.

STRUCTURE: A wine's "architecture." Typically, flavor, acidity, and tannins come together to give a sense of a wine's "bones," or how a wine is put together. A well-structured wine will often age well, although it can also be drunk immediately in many cases.

TANNIN: A component in red wines that comes mainly from the skins and seeds during maceration, a period before fermentation from grape juice to wine. Tannin makes your cheeks feel prickly and often indicates that a wine has aging potential (wine critics will sometimes commend a tannic wine for its "structure"). Of course, when tannin is totally out of balance with the fruit in a wine, it can mean that the wine was crudely made. A heavily tannic wine isn't much fun to drink: it turns your tongue to leather.

TERROIR: A French concept that basically indicates an ineffable combination of soil, sun, and the spirit of a particular place. Essentially, it means that the region where a grape was made is reflected in the final, bottled product.

VARIETY/VARIETAL: Grapes come in varieties; wines come in varietals. When Merlot is a grape, it's a variety. When it's a bottled wine, it's a varietal. Easy as that.

VINIFERA: Vinifera grapes are of the so-called "noble" varieties: Cabernet Sauvignon, Chardonnay, Merlot, and so on. They generally produce higher-quality wines than non-vinifera grapes. American native varietals are all non-vinifera.

VINTAGE: A vintage wine is simply a wine that has a date on it. All wines that bear a vintage must have been made from grapes harvested that year. Nonvintage wines are not so constrained. They can be blended from wines of different years. This isn't as big a deal as it sounds—nonvintage wines can also be excellent. Champagne, for example, is often a nonvintage wine.

VITICULTURE: This is the entire system of wine-grape cultivation, from preparing the vineyards to pruning the vines to establishing leaf canopies and trellising schemes. Viticulture involves the decision whether or not to use pesticides, whether to harvest by machine or by hand, whether to irrigate, and so on. Viticulture is usually a collaboration among the owner of the winery, the winemaker, and the vineyard manager, who looks after the vines. In up-and-coming American wine regions, these three are often the same person.

ACKNOWLEDGMENTS

BOOKS ARE NOT SOLO EFFORTS. For this one, I'm grateful to my agent at Sanford J. Greenburger Associates, Dan Mandel; my editor, Chris Steighner, for his patience and talent; Allison Williams, who whipped the thing into shape; Kathleen Jayes, who brought me to Rizzoli in the first place; *Wine Spectator*'s James Molesworth, with whom I tasted many, many, *many* regional American wines in 2002; and all the wine pros who have helped me out over the years, with both sustenance and conversation, especially Delphine Boutier, Lawrence Osborne, Catherine Miles, Adrian Bridge, Pierre-Henry Gagey, Christopher Shipley, Shelley Clark, Michelle and Carlo Pulixi, and Anthony Cerbone.

But of course deepest thanks should go to America's regional winemakers. To name only a few: Bunny and Dr. Richard Becker; Jim and Karen Johnson; Tom and Marti Macinski; Richard Olsen-Harbich; Roman Roth, Bruce Schneider and Christiane Baker Schneider; and Jim and Debra Vascik. A nod as well to Patricia and Robert Vander Lyn.

Of course, it was ultimately the strength of family that made everything possible. A toast to Mario and Jacqueline Russo, John Russo, Mel Russo, Mark and Carol DeBord, and Nora DeBord. And to my wife, Maria, the look of love, always.

—MATTHEW DEBORD

PHOTO CREDITS

Adelsheim Vineyard: 146, 158, 159; Argyle Winery: 150; Barboursville: vii, 68, 74, 79, 80; Robert Baumgardner: vi, 104, 107, 112, 114, 117, 118; Beaulieu Vineyard: 193; Bedell: 18; Bel Lago: 96; Marc Bennett: 109; Brent Bergherm: 164, 174, 176; Bernardus Lodge: 189; Biltmore Estate, Asheville, NC: 71, 83; Black Star Farms: 92; Blue Mountain Vineyards/Vicki Greff: 60; Brandywine River Museum: 52; Breaux Vineyards: 81; Canyon Wind Cellars: 134; Chaddsford Winery: 59; Chateau Fontaine: 97; Chehalem Wines: 152, 153; Clos Pegase: 187, 201; Clover Hill: 54, 61; Dan Coffey/ Colorado Wine Industry Development Board: cover, 124, 130; Colorado Cellars: 129, 135; Corning Museum of Glass: 33; Brian Coufer, Studio B Photography: 91, 99; Domaine Carneros: 190; Domaine Chandon: 194; Tom Donohue /Montauk Point Lighthouse: 10; Joe Duty: 177; Dick Erath: 154; Owen Franken/CORBIS: 111; Fulton Davenport: 106; Geneva On the Lake: 34; Grand Junction Visitor & Convention Bureau: 126, 127, 128; Graystone Winery: 132; Great Lakes Culinary Institute: 90; Mike Haverkate/Vista Balloon: 143; The Hess Collection: 202; Hotel Oregon: 144; Diane Huntress/Plum Creek Cellars: 133; Inn at Little Washington: 73; Kirk Irwin: 192, 195, 196; Linden Vineyards: 76; Matthew Mahon: 115; Maidstone Arms: 13; Sara Matthews: 14, 16, 20, 24, 148, 147; John McJunkin/Cayuse Vineyards: 170, 173; Messina Hof: 119; Bill Milne/Wölffer Vineyards: 8, 11, 23; Monticello/Thomas Jefferson Foundation, Inc.: 70; R & K Muschenetz/Cephas: 116; Ponzi Vineyards: 150; Raphael Winery: 19; Kristian S. Reynolds: 30, 32, 35, 36, 38, 39, 40, 41, 42, 43, 44, 45; John Rizzo: 154; Mick Rock/Cephas: 50, 53, 56, 57, 58; Steve Sadler: 88, 91, 94; St. Supery Vineyards: 200; John Scriver: 182, 198, 199; Seven Springs Resort: 55; Smithbridge/Jim Esham: 63; Sokol Blosser: 155; Jim Stranahan: 167, 175; Strawberry Canyon Lodge: 168; Sutter Home Winery: 203; John Valls/Ponzi Vineyards: 151; Vynecrest Vineyards and Winery: 62; Whitman Mission Natural Historic Site: 166, 169; MJ Wickham/Copia: 186; Joseph A. Wiencko, Jr.: 77, 78; Doreen Wunja/Chehalem Wines: 142; Doreen Wunja/Domaine Drouhin: 140, 157, back cover.

SCHEDULE OF FESTIVALS

CALIFORNIA
Napa Valley Wine Auction
June
St. Helena
707-963-3388

Wine Country Film Festival
Summer
Glen Ellen
707-935-FILM

COLORADO
Colorado Mountain WineFest
September
Riverbend Park
Palisade
800-962-2547

Food and Wine Classic
June
Aspen
877-900-WINE
www.foodandwine.com

MICHIGAN
Traverse Epicurean Classic
October
Traverse City
231-932-0475
www.epicureanclassic.com

NEW YORK
Finger Lakes Wine Festival
July
Watkins Glen
607-535-2481

Harvest Party
October
Wölffer Estate
631-537-5106

Long Island Wine Classic
August
Bridgehampton
631-537-3177

Toast To The East End: Wine,
Auction, and Dinner
September
East Wind Caterers
Wading River
516-827-1290

OREGON
Memorial Weekend in the
Wine Country
May
Yamhill County
503-646-2985
www.yamhillwine.com

Oregon Pinot Camp
June
North Willamette Valley
503-292-0272
www.oregonpinotcamp.com

PENNSYLVANIA
Great Tastes of Pennsylvania
Wine & Food Festival
June
Split Rock Resort
Harmony
800-255-7625

Seven Springs Wine & Food
Festival
August
Seven Springs Resort
Champion
800-452-2223

TEXAS
Saveur Hill Country Wine &
Food Festival
April
Austin
512-542-WINE
www.texaswineandfood.org

VIRGINIA
VWGA Virginia Wine Festival
August
Historical Long Branch Farm
Millwood
800-277-2675
www.showsinc.com

Vintage Virginia Festival
June
Historic Long Branch Farm
Millwood
800-277-2675
www.showsinc.com

WASHINGTON
Northwest Wine & Food Festival
August
Seattle
425-603-9558
www.enosoc.org

LISTING OF STORES

In some cases, wineries can ship wines across the country, though regulations vary by state. Here are some wine stores that specialize in the wines of their regions:

CALIFORNIA
K&L Wine Merchants
638 Fourth Street
San Francisco, CA 94107
415-896-1734
www.klwines.com

K&L Wine Merchants
3005 El Camino Real
Redwood City, CA 94061
650-364-8544
Famous nationwide for its outstanding selection, which includes the best California has to offer.

Wally's
2107 Westwood Boulevard
Los Angeles, CA 90025
888-9-WALLYS
wallywine.com
The best wine store in Los Angeles, Wally's has a selection of notable California bottlings that is second to none.

COLORADO
Andy's Liquor Mart
922 North First Street
Grand Junction, CO 81501
970-243-1176

ILLINOIS
Sam's Wine & Spirits
1720 North Marcey Street
Chicago, IL 60514
630-705-9463
samswine.com

Sam's Wine & Spirits
2010 Butterfield Road
Downers Grove, IL 60515
630-705-9463
These mega-stores are the best Windy City places to shop for wines.

MICHIGAN
Jack's Market
448 E. Front Street
Traverse City, MI 49684
231-947-6170
Conveniently located in Traverse City, smack in the middle of Northern Michigan wine country, Jack's is where you can find L. Mawby's lineup of sparkling wines, close to the source.

Merchant's Fine Wine
22250 Michigan Avenue
Dearborn, MI 48124
313-563-8700
merchantsfinewine.com

NEW YORK
Red, White & Bubbly
211 5th Avenue
Brooklyn, NY 11217
718-636-9463
Located in one of the hippest neighborhoods in Brooklyn, this well-stocked store carries plenty of wines from Long Island's North Fork.

Vintage New York
482 Broome Street
New York, NY 10013
212-226-9463
vintagenewyork.com

Vintage New York
2492 Broadway
New York, NY 10025
212-721-9999

Vintage New York at
Rivendell Winery
714 Albany Post Road
New Paltz, New York 12561
845-255-2494
rivendellwine.com
There are now three locations for this enterprise, which offers the most comprehensive selection of New York State wines anywhere. Because the owners operate a winery, the stores by law are allowed to be open seven days a week (everyone else is limited to six).

OREGON
Liner & Elsen
202 NW 21st Avenue
Portland, OR 97209
800-903-WINE
linerandelsen.com
This well-regarded Portland shop carries an extensive selection of Oregon Pinot Noirs.

PENNSYLVANIA
Chaddsford At Exton Mall
Exton Square Mall
Routes 30 & 100
Exton, PA 19341
610-524-5450

Chaddsford At Springfield Mall
Springfield Mall
1250 Baltimore Pike
Springfield, PA 19064
610-544-8776
Pennsylvania's best-known winery operates several satellite locations away from the winery. At these sites, curious consumers can taste the best the Keystone State has to offer.

Wine & Spirits Store
5430 Centre Avenue
Pittsburgh, PA 15232
412-688-1938

Wine & Spirits Store
1218 Chestnut Street
Philadelphia, PA 19107-5410
215-560-4380
The Pennsylvania Liquor Control Board licenses numerous stores throughout the state that sell Pennsylvania regional wines from wineries such as Chaddsford and Blue Mountain. These two stores carry the PLCB's Premium Collection, which can also be perused online at pawineandspirits.com.

TEXAS
The Grapevine
1612 Hunter Road
New Braunfels, TX 78130
830-606-0093
This store in the San Antonio area maintains a large selection of Texas wines, from wineries such as Llano Estacado and Fall Creek.

VIRGINIA
Made In Virginia Store
807 Caroline Street
Fredericksburg, Virginia 22401
540-371-2030
800-635-3149
madeinva.com
In addition to carrying numerous local products on its website, Made In Virginia also operates a store in historic Fredericksburg. Look for wines from Barboursville, the state's best-known winery.

The Wine Specialist
2115 M Street NW
Washington, DC 20037
800-832-0704
202-833-9507
Virginia wines are carried at this store in the nearby nation's capital.

WASHINGTON
Pike & Western Wine Shop
1934 Pike Place
Seattle, WA 98101
206-441-1307
Open since the mid-1970s, this Seattle store has grown up alongside the state's burgeoning wine industry. A great resource for the wines of Washington.

INDEX

(Page numbers in *italic* refer to illustrations. Page numbers in lighter type refer to maps.)

A

Adelsheim Vineyard, *146,* 149, 158, *158, 159, 160*
    Oregon Pinot Noir, 161
Alamosa Wine Cellars, 113, *114,* 115, *115*
    El Guapo, 120
    Viognier, 120
Allegro Vineyards, *56*
Argyle Winery, *147, 148,* 149, 150, *150*
    "Nuthouse" Pinot Noir, 160
    Pinot Noir, 160

B

Barboursville Vineyards, *viii, 68,* 75, *79,* 79–81, *80, 84, 85*

Brut, 85
Cabernet Franc, 85
Viognier Reserve, 84–85
Beaulieu Vineyard, 191, 193, *193*
    Georges de Latour Private Reserve Cabernet Sauvignon, 204
Beaux Frères Vineyard Pinot Noir, 2, 161, *161*
Becker Vineyards, 113, *116,* 117, *117, 120, 121*
    Cabernet-Syrah, 121
    Vintage Port Estate Bottled, 2, 120
Bedell Cellars, 15, 17–19, *18, 26*
    C-Block South Merlot, 26
    Main Road Red, 26
Bel Lago Winery, 95, 96, *96, 101*
    Pinot Grigio, 101
Beringer Vineyards, 191, *192,* 193–94
    Private Reserve Napa Valley Cabernet Sauvignon, 205

Biltmore Estate, *71,* 75, 82, *83, 85*
    Cabernet Sauvignon, 85
Blue Mountain Vineyards, 57, 60, *60, 64*
    Blue Heron Meritage, 64
    Ice Wine, 64–65
Bonny Doon/Ca' Del Solo Big House Red, *204,* 205
Breaux Vineyards, 75, 81, *81*

C

Canyon Wind Cellars, 131, 134, *134, 136*
    Desert Rosé, 136
    Merlot, 136
Castello di Borghese Vineyard & Winery, 15, *16,* 17
Cayuse Vineyards, *170,* 171, 172, *173, 178*
    Cailloux Syrah, 178
Chaddsford Winery, 57, *58,* 59, *59,* 64, 65
    Cabernet/Chambourcin, 64

Miller Estate Vineyard Chardonnay, 64
Philip Roth Vineyard Chardonnay, 2, 64
Channing Daughters, 15, 24, *26*
"The Sculptor" Merlot, 26
Chateau de Leelanau, 95, 97
Andante, 101
Chateau Fontaine, 95, 97, *97, 101*
Pinot Gris, 101
Chateau Ste. Michelle:
Blanc de Blanc, 179
Cabernet Sauvignon, 179
Chehalem, *142*, 149, *152*, 153, *153*
Clos Pegase, *187*, 191, 201, *201*
Hommage Cabernet Sauvignon, 205
Clover Hill Vineyards and Winery, *54*, 57, *61*, 61–62, *65*
Generations Chardonnay, 65
Generations Riesling, 65
Colorado Cellars Winery, *129*, 131, 135, *135*
Chardonnay, 137
Columbia Crest Chardonnay, 179

D

Domaine Carneros, *190*
Domaine Chandon, 191, 194, *194, 207*
Brut Classic, 207
Domaine Drouhin Oregon, 149, 156, *157*
Pinot Noir, 160
Duck Walk Vineyards, 15, 24, *24*
Dunham Cellars, 172

E

Erath Vineyards, 149, 154, *154, 160*
Pinot Noir, 160

F

Fall Creek Vineyards, 113, 118, *120*
Meritus, 120
Reserve Chardonnay, 120
Fox Run Vineyards, 37, *38, 39,* 39–40, *46*
Cabernet Franc, 46
Dry Riesling, 46

G

Gallo of Sonoma Chardonnay, 206
Galluccio Family Wineries, *14*, 15, *20*, 21–22
Good Harbor Vineyards, 95, 98
Graystone Winery, 131, 132, *132, 137*
Port, 137

H

Hess Collection, 191, 202, *202*
Hogue Cellars, *167*, 171, 175, *175, 178*
Gewürztraminer, 178
Johannisberg Riesling, 178

L

Lamoreaux Landing Wine Cellars, *35*, 37, *40, 40, 41, 47*
Dry Riesling, 47
Pinot Noir, 47
Lawrence, M., *100*
Sex Brut Rosé, 101

U.S. Brut, 100
L'Ecole No. 41 Winery, *164, 174*, 175, *178*
Seven Hills Vineyard Merlot, 178
Lenz, 15, 21, *27*
Estate Selection Merlot, 26
Leonetti:
Cabernet Sauvignon, 179
Merlot, 2, 179
Leorie Vineyard, *94*
Linden Vineyards, 75, 76, *76, 84*
Hardscrabble Chardonnay, 84
Hardscrabble Red, 84
Llano Estacado Shiraz, 121, *121*

M

Mawby, L., Vineyards, *91*, 95, 98–99, *99, 100*
Blanc de Blanc, 2, 100
Blanc de Noir, 100
Redd, 100
Messina Hof Winery & Resort, 113, 119, *119*
White Zinfandel, 121
Mondavi, Robert, Winery, 191, 195, *195*
Cabernet Sauvignon Reserve, 2, 204

N

Naylor Wine Cellars, *53*
Niebaum-Coppola, 191, 197–98, *198, 199*
Rosso, 205

O

Opus One, 191, *196*, 197, *204*, 205

P

Pepperwood Grove Pinot Noir, 204, *204*

Plum Creek Cellars, 131, 133, *133, 137*

    Cabernet Franc, 2, 136–37

    Reserve Cabernet Sauvignon, 137

Ponzi Vineyards, 149, 151, *151, 160*

    Pinot Noir Reserve, 160

R

Raphael, 15, 19, *19, 27*

    Merlot, 26

    Sauvignon Blanc, 26

Red Newt Cellars, 37, 44, *44, 45, 46*

    Riesling Dry Reserve, 2, 46

    Riesling Semi-Dry, 46

Rex Hill Pinot Noir, 161, *161*

S

St. Supéry Vineyards and Winery, 191, 200, *200*

    Cabernet Sauvignon, 207

Schneider Vineyards, 15, 25

    Cabernet Franc, 27

Potato Barn Red, 27

Shaw, Charles, Cabernet Sauvignon, 206, *206*

Smithbridge Cellars, 57, 63, *63*

    Sweet Riesling, 65

Snoqualmie Vineyards, *178*

    Cabernet Sauvignon, 179

Sokol Blosser Winery, 149, 155, *155*

    Willamette Valley Pinot Noir, 161

Spicewood Vineyards, *vi–vii*

Stag's Leap Cask 23 Estate Cabernet Sauvignon, 206, *207*

Standing Stone Vineyards, 37, *42,* 43, *43*

    Gewürztraminer, 47

    Riesling, 46

Sutter Home Winery, 191, 203, *203*

    White Zinfandel, 206

Swanson Vineyards Alexis, 207

T

Three Rivers Winery, 171, 176, *176*

    Columbia Valley Cabernet Sauvignon, 178

Two Rivers Winery, 131, 132, *136*

    Chardonnay, 136

    Riesling, 136

V

Valhalla Vineyards, 75, *77,* 77–78, *78*

    Gotterdammerung, 2, 84

    Syrah, 84

Vynecrest Winery, 57, 62, *62*

    Riesling, 65

W

Walla Walla Vintners, 171, 177, *177*

    Columbia Valley Cabernet Sauvignon, 178

Wiemer, Hermann J.:

    Dry Johannisberg Riesling Reserve, 47

    Select Late Harvest Ice Wine, 47, *47*

Wölffer, *8, 11,* 15, 22, *23, 27*

    Estate Selection Chardonnay, 2, 27